He HEALS the HURT

SHARON M. STONE

BLUEPRINT PRESS
INTERNATIONALE

ISBN
978-1-959365-34-1 (Paperback)
978-1-959365-35-8 (eBook)
978-1-959365-33-4 (Hardcover)

To Abba Father, who cared enough to rescue me and eradicate all my hurt and pain.

To Yeshua (Jesus), our High Priest after the order of Melchizedek, who has been tried on all points, bears all our sickness, disease, iniquities, pains, sorrows, and griefs.

He alone who has the power to save, change, transform, shift, lift, renew, restore, and make us whole again.

To the Holy Ghost, who comes alongside us and dwells within to comfort, keep, guide, and apply the ointment to our wounds.

TABLE OF CONTENTS

ACKNOWLEDGMENTS

This special acknowledgment goes to all those who have helped me through encouraging words, prayers, or have shown themselves true friends throughout the process of the completion of this book, those who have given me that extra push to get the job done.

Those who have proofed this book or been used by God to give me greater insight on what I needed to expand and expound upon in this book, I greatly thank you all: Prophet Eddie Wright Jr., Prophetess Rowena Welch (Tulsa, Oklahoma), Bishop V. S. Beckford Sr. (my father) and Lady R. V. Beckford (my mother) of Georgian Hills Church of God, the late Mother Lea Lawson (Montgomery, Alabama), Jill Gill, Anita White, Prophetess Wanda K. Griffin, Apostle Benny Mbai of Generation Changers (Kenya, Africa), Prophetess Gwendolyn Simpson, the late Bishop Rodger Gumm, Apostle Felix Beale (both of Chicago, Illinois), Pastor FW McCoy (New York, New York), Prophet Robert Mallard (Los Angeles, California), Prophet George Culley (Pinckneyville, Illinois), Apostle Kenneth Brewer, and the many other vessels God used to encourage, lift, and shift me into position. Thank you for blessing me with your love, prayers, and words!

A special thanks to the late Dr. Binford Peeples, for words of encouragement, faith, confidence, and love; I was honored to be acquainted with you and grew to know you in the Lord.

A very special thanks to my dear son and daughter, retired Gunny Sergeant Johnathan and Horquidea Beckford for sowing into me and making this publication a reality and no longer a dream. The Lord bless you richly.

To the many souls who have purchased, read, and partaken of this book and received their healing and deliverance, been made perfectly whole, and set free from all that had hindered, obstructed, and bound them from going forth and living life more abundantly: "You are healed in Jesus' name, amen!" Thank you greatly for your support!

Note to the reader: Though this book contains a vast amount of scriptural references, it is by no means a substitute for daily reading of the Word of God (the Holy Bible), which is the sword of the Spirit!

So arm yourself likewise by reading the Word of God, renewing your mind in His holy ways daily!

PREFACE

In our society, we find many people are hurting. This was also true of the people throughout the Bible. It does not matter whether we are of a particular race, color, creed, cultural background, or ethnic group. Whether we are rich or poor, of the working class, or unemployed, some form of hurt will find you. Hurt will come when you least expect it. It's like a heat-seeking missile that torpedoes its way into your life, piercing your very heart with its icy and sometimes fatal blow. There are as many ways to hurt someone as there are many kinds of hurt. There is only one true and permanent remedy for hurt, but the best way to be healed is when there is release, as when the Savior, Christ himself, comes in and saturates your life with His love, seemingly melting away or erasing hurt. What a joy!

One can be hurt by an enemy, a stranger, but it is more likely the one that you love the most always seem to hurt you the worst. We are sometimes hurt on our jobs, by close friends, our relatives, the church we may attend, even our acquaintances, yet some of us never learn to or refuse to *forgive*. Learn to let it go. (We'll discuss forgiveness and letting go in later chapters.) Jesus instructed us to forgive those who offend or transgress against us (i.e., those who sin or do wrong) seventy times seven, which simply means, as often as we are offended (wronged), we must forgive. (Read Luke 17:3-4.) You might say that's easier said than done, but by initiating and employing forgiveness, you take away the power from that person or thing that has a crushing hold over your life! Flip the script, so to speak (use reverse psychology) by asking them to forgive you, even if you weren't the violator but the one violated or transgressed against. This will defuse the atmosphere and confuse your adversary. Then you'll go from a casualty to a victor. Once you do this, you'll feel the weight of the world roll off your shoulders. Consider these words (written on July 25, 2001) the next time you feel it's hard to let go:

A Prayer of Forgiveness

Forgive me if I have said words that do pierce and do cut real deep
Forgive me if I sometimes don't see eye to eye with you
Forgive me if I in some way have stepped upon your toes
Forgive if unintentionally I've caused you hurt or pain
Forgive me if unknowingly I've brought to your name some kind of shame
Forgive me if somehow I've caused your radiant countenance to be down
Forgive me if I made you cry because my actions caused a rift somehow
And if something I said or done has caused your soul to be unquiet.
Forgive me, sometimes I cannot see because I'm standing too close to the tree.
Forgive me for the times I appear less human, not showing any empathy.
Forgive me if I don't feel wrong, and upon my convictions I stand real strong.
Forgive me if I did yell, and in your heart it felt I swelled.
Forgive me for feeling offended and becoming rather defensive.
Forgive me for upholding what I know, for that's how the story goes.
Forgive if it felt to you like I've slapped you in the face.
Forgive if it seems I am removed and placed our relationship upon a shelf.
Forgive me if it seems to you I've lied, cheated some way, or connived.
Forgive me if I disillusioned your perspective concerning me.
May God help us, my friend, to clearly see.
Forgive me if I to you seem to be a loner,
When all you desired to do was to fellowship with your sister or your brother.
Forgive me if I to you have shown myself less than a friend.
Forgive me if I've allowed the devil to come in.
Forgive me if with my voice harsh tones I did rend, when subtlety was needed to mend.
Forgive me if I allowed self to rise up, and to the mind of Christ, I did not bend.
Forgive me if it seems I'm not in right standing with you.

When we are able to forgive, certain things occur. There is reconciliation (adjustment), restoration (brought back into agreement), and redemption (being set free). For us, Jesus is the Great Mediator, the Advocate between God the Father and man, the One reconciling us back to our rightful place in His kingdom as children, then heirs of God and joint heirs with Christ. We who are believers have received the Spirit of adoption.

> *Certain things occur when we are able to forgive:*
>
> *Reconcile vb -ciled, -ciling*
>
> *1: to cause to be friendly or harmonious again*
>
> *2: ADJUST, SETTLE <~differences~>*
>
> *3: to bring to submission or acceptance Concilate 1: to bring into agreement 2: to gain the good will of: accommodate, conform —1.1-*

For as many as are led by the Spirit of God, they are the sons of God. For ye have not received the spirit of bondage again to fear: but ye have received the Spirit of adoption, whereby we cry, Abba, Father. The Spirit itself beareth witness with our spirit, that we are the children of God: And if children, then heirs; heirs of God, and joint-heirs with Christ; if so be that we suffer with him, that we may be also glorified together. *(Rom. 8:14-17; KJV)*

Love covers a multitude of sins (faults, wrongdoings). We will remain hindered if we never allow the sweet-smelling savor of His love to come in to cover, lift, unshackle, undo, and separate us from our past hurts. This keeps us from forgiving, and it will surely keep us out of God's presence and kingdom.

Won't you allow the Savior to baptize you in His love and wash away all the hurt that's within? Because of Christ the Messiah, we are no longer enslaved to sin, death, or pain. He BORE IT ALL because of His great ever-abounding love, so as you read the pages of this book, I sincerely hope that you too would come to know Him (Jesus) who bore all pain, sorrow, and grief for us and that you would come to know that HE HEALS THE HURT!

Note to Reader:** Though this book contains a vast amount of scriptural references, it is **by no means** and **on no certain terms** a **substitute** for daily reading of the **Word of God** (The Holy Bible), which is the **Sword of the Spirit!

So arm yourself likewise by reading the Word of God, renewing your mind in His holy ways daily!

INTRODUCTION

It was in 1995 that God began me on a wonderful journey of writing this book. This came a few years after dealing with the tragedy of my fiancé's (Karlton Lawson's) life coming to an end on October 4, 1990. I experienced the collapse of what seemed to be my world as I knew it; it all came crashing in. When I received the call about his death, it was one of the most heart-wrenching things I've had to experience. His life expired after suffering from sarcoidosis. Sarcoidosis is a disease of unknown cause that leads to inflammation and it affects your body's organs.

I had endured the loss of a child, but this was totally a different kind of loss. I lost my best friend, my love, my confidant, my soulmate. I didn't get the chance to say goodbye. That was a painful and harsh reality to accept, painful because I'd made a promise to Karlton and harsh because I couldn't keep it.

After his funeral, I was constantly being told I had to be strong for Mother (Dr. Marjore Lea Lawson, Karlton's mom), the children (my sons, Bryan and Johnathan), and the family, but no one considered me. They didn't consider that I myself was barely holding on, They didn't consider that I needed to weep, release, and be restored. This put me in a perplexed state. Being highly exasperated, I went back to work thinking I could escape what I was feeling if I kept occupied; it didn't help! Matter of fact, it seemed to make the situation worse. I would find myself sobbing uncontrollably for hours. It was hurtful to see someone who was wearing a wedding or engagement ring or to even listen to music that we'd once shared. The pain was sometimes debilitating, it seemed. We had plans that would never be fulfilled. It felt like I was left hanging. I almost lost sight of my purpose for living. There were some who empathized with me while others felt the need to preach to and at me, telling me to stop crying. They had no idea the depth of my hurt or why I was hurting. I just wanted to be left alone.

My children (who were only seven and eleven at the time) suffered because their mother became incapable of dealing with her pain, hurt, sorrow, and grief. Where they once knew me as being very warm, inviting, and affectionate, with each passing day I became more and more withdrawn and indifferent. Depression found me despite how much Word (scripture) I thought I knew. It found me despite my being an anointed vessel. It took hold of me despite the closeness I believed I had in my walk with God. I was growing despondent until my sons left me a letter. I was failing them. I wasn't being their mom, and I needed to know that they were hurting too. They'd lost their dad. I had almost forgotten that they loved Karlton as well.

I knew I couldn't stay in that place of hopelessness. It appeared I was literally caught between a rock and a hard place. Not only did I struggle with Karlton's death, but other issues from past hurts and pains surfaced. Those things I thought I'd released (gave them to God but hadn't really dealt with or processed) prior to his death rushed to the forefront of my mind and heart. There was deep-seated despair, sexual frustration (my flesh longed, desired to be touched, held), emotional tumult (my emotions were raging), and spiritual disconnect; it was all sheer and utter chaos. I went on a spiritual, emotional, and mental roller coaster ride. At that time I was like these words in this poem I wrote on April 13, 1999:

Struggle

We struggle through our woes, our aches and our pains
Hoping for some kind of relief to show up in our lives
Abolishing the agony and strain.
We wear many hats and sometimes many masks too.
Needless to say what is relief if we have no peace.
And what is having all things if in life
we lose that which we gain.
Juggling from day to day, unsure of our own
destiny, wondering how it will all end.
The course we choose sometimes
brings us to our wit's end.
Striving, searching for whom we can depend.
My message strong and prolonged as it
resounds to each of you today:
Look up for your redemption draweth nigh.
See God's blessings all around, brand-
new mercies coming your way.
Then there'll be no more struggles for you and me
If this you remember well that the battle
is not yours, it is the Lord's.

The Father administered healing to me, even when all I wanted to do was withdraw within myself and shut down. I am thankful that God is omnipotent (He reigns with infinite power), omnipresent (ever-present, all-dwelling), omniscient (all-knowing, has infinite knowledge), and that He is ever mindful of me, and I am so glad that God's word is true!

Like the scripture said in Isaiah 59:19 (AMP), "When the enemy shall come in, like a flood; the Spirit of the Lord will lift up a standard against him and put him to flight [for He will come like a rushing stream which the breath of the Lord drives]." Just think of it. Whenever the enemy shows up, that's when the Holy Spirit comes to our aid. He lifts up the word against our adversary, the devil. I am thankful He rushes in to our defense. Aren't you?

God met me at the point of no return while I was seemingly going through another shutdown. From November 1990 to 1993, God washed me with his word, applied ointment to my wounds, and salted me with his love, forgiveness, joy, peace, faithfulness, long-suffering, goodness, gentleness, kindness, meekness, and temperance (self-control). I am tremendously blessed to have loving, caring, and praying people in my life too. Through God's reconciliation for my life, He has erased, removed, lifted, shifted, restored, renewed, delivered, and *healed* the hurt!

CHAPTER 1

WHAT HURT US

Hurt does not care about the age of its target. Neither do we know how it shall come or in what form. Think about it: Yesterday's hurts are today's pain and tomorrow's woe. If we are not careful, we will make yesterday's mistake by not resolving today's problem, which turn into tomorrow's failures (shortcomings). Remember, the chain is only as strong as its weakest link. You don't have to be victimized. In Christ we are made more than conquerors through his love *(Rom. 8:37 KJV)*.

When we are hurt because of failed dreams, deflated expectations, unfulfilled desires, it gets perverted as unfiltered anger. Pent-up anger can turn to bitterness and cankerous rage. Possibly, it is from the loss of something or someone most precious. Maybe you've been sifted by an unforeseen accident that left your body twisted, disfigured, mangled, even paralyzed. The diagnosis? You'll never walk again, never have the use of your limbs, never fully recover from this misfortunate event, or you'll be a vegetable. Maybe you were contemptuously manipulated, only to have your hopes dashed and your dreams shattered. Maybe it is one heartbreak after another or disappointment from a promise that was broken. Presumably, there is the inability to make commitment. Possibly you have become overly cautious, irritated, disgusted, and frustrated after being floored by infidelity, or you are dealt the blow of a failed relationship. Perhaps it is rejection. You play the blame game, but that gets you nowhere. You are still hurt! How you respond to the hurt makes all the difference to your outcome.

What hurt us is sin and its devices: the spirit of jealousy, envy, and strife, the spirit of malice, hatred, murder, and wrath, the lust of the flesh (lewdness, fornication, uncleanness), the lust of the eye (covetousness), and the pride of life (being high-minded, stiff-necked, and having a proud look, as well as taking the Living God and privileges for granted). This is the spirit of witchcraft: rebellion and idolatry, stubbornness that derives from pride. No matter what direction it comes from or what form it takes on or appears as, our hurt, pain, and grief can come upon us because of sin, sin in our lives or in the lives of those who inflict or prey upon others. The Bible warns us about following after such things that can cause us to walk in discord. Discord not only hurts but takes us out of fellowship with God and others.

These six things the Lord hates, indeed seven are an abomination to Him: A proud look [the spirit that makes one overestimate himself and underestimate others], a lying tongue, and hands that shed innocent blood. *(Ref: Ps. 120:2-3, AMP)*

A heart that manufactures wicked thoughts and plans, feet that are swift in running evil, A false witness who breathes out lies [even under oath], and he who sows discord among his brethren. *(Prov. 6:16-19, AMP)*

This is the message which we have heard from Him and declare to you, that God is light and in Him is no darkness at all. If we say that we have fellowship with Him, and walk in darkness, we lie and do not practice the truth. But if we walk in the light, we have fellowship with one another, and the blood of Jesus Christ His Son cleanses us from all sin. *(1 John 1:5-7, NKJV)*

God not only hates it, he also says that discord is an abomination to him. It is so because it pathologically seeks to divide and conquer. The spirit of discord causes us to have friction with one another. It causes conflict, strife, disunity, variance, and warfare amongst us. It not only causes alienation, isolation, and separation from others but also cuts us off from God. When we walk in discord and not in love, we will always clash, collide, and compete with each other because there is a lack of harmony and unity. This atmosphere causes warfare, and warfare always brings with it death.

Ever turn to the church and felt you were being ostracized? This is where we get the term *church hurt* from. You confide in someone within the body of Christ only to find that they have put you out on front street, or you go to your leaders and find that in the next service that what you have divulged in discretion is now aired over the pulpit. What you thought was taken to God in prayer became news for all and caused you great shame and pain. Maybe you were violated by the one who was your covering. Now you are left devastated by their actions and perhaps are turning or have turned your back on God. Perhaps you have left the church because of it. Church hurt is a place that causes one to lose sight of faith, trust, fellowship, and respect for the leadership in church, as well as others in Christianity and the body of Christ as a whole. And like I said previously, it can even cause you to withdraw from God as if he were the blame for it.

Here's a life experience: When I was in college, my eldest brother suffered with Crohn's disease and was hospitalized for over twenty-one days at one time. I went one evening to relieve my mother, who stayed at his bedside so she could sleep at least one night in her own bed. While I was there that evening, one of the elders close to our family came to visit him. As the elder was preparing to leave, my brother went to the bathroom. Now I know the Word says that we are to greet one another with a holy kiss, but that's not what he did.

He took advantage of the timing and tried to forcefully kiss me, scrubbing my face and lips with his bristly unshaven beard. My lips and the right side of my face became swollen from the irritation. I was shocked, stunned even to think that someone I had looked up to and respected would attempt to do such things, that someone I had experienced and seen the move of God upon would allow their flesh to override them, that they would disrespect and disregard any disapproval of their actions. I guess that is why the scriptures says "It is better to *take refuge* in the Lord than to trust in man" *(Ps. 118:8, KWSB; italics added)* and "Do not *put* your *trust* in princes, in *mortal men*, who cannot save" *(Ps. 146:3, KWSB; italics added).*

I called my big sister (in the Lord) Anita and asked what should I do. I wasn't sure how to tell my parents about this ordeal or how they would respond since this was their friend that made this infraction on me, especially since by this time I was already a teenaged mother. It did not matter that I had my life back on track with God. The enemy came at me hard through this. It caused me to withdraw from not only men but women as well. I felt violated. I felt that if this was Christianity, then I did not want it. Have you ever had an instance in the church that pushed you to this place?

Oh, I still attended service, taught Sunday School, was the choir director and the minister of music. But as soon as worship service was over, I would bypass everyone and go straight to the car without really speaking or fellowshipping, no matter how close someone was to me. Despite my behavior behind this, I still loved God. I still wanted to please God and serve him with my all. My problem was I had lost all faith and trust in people. It bothered me every time this elder would come to worship with us. I did not want to be touched by anyone and made the decision to get some pleasure for myself without regard for others. I would do to men what they had done to me: use them. I would do my thing, repent (sometimes while on the way to service), and earnestly pray and ask God the Father not to expose or uncover me. Sounds crazy, doesn't it? I would even ask Him to save me from myself. Guess what, He actually did, and the Lord kept me from open shame. He didn't allow me to give his kingdom a black eye. He also did not let me slide in the things I was involved with.

The scripture says, "For whom the Lord loves he chastens, and scourges every son whom he receives" *(Heb, 12:6, NKJV).*

The Lord dealt with me about what I was doing because I was not operating truly in His perfect will but in the permissive. The Holy Ghost brought the error of my ways to my attention. I wanted God's hands on my life, not off. I needed the Father's presence, the stability of his peace and comfort of his love. I wanted to be in God's perfect will, so I had to let go any resentment I had toward this elder and anyone else I felt had hurt me at this point. I came to terms with what I was doing and surrendered to the Lord the frustration and unforgiveness I had harbored.

One day, I heard that this elder was gravely ill; it pricked my heart. It was only then that I was able to ask God to heal and have mercy upon him. That is when I knew that the Lord truly healed me from this thing called church hurt. I didn't tell anyone what I was dealing with but Jesus. Frankly, I didn't tell it because I did not believe anyone but God cared. I am so glad I now know what I did not seem to know then, that there are those who we can share with who will help us past ourselves, that there are those who will pray for us and not condemn us, those who will strengthen us through God's word, love, and peace with the joy of salvation, and those who will weep with us when we weep and rejoice with us when we rejoice.

The apostle James said we are to be able to confess and pray for one another that we may be healed.

> And the prayer of faith shall save the sick, and the Lord shall raise him up; and if he have committed sins, they shall be forgiven him. Confess your faults one to another, and pray one for another, that ye may be healed. The effectual fervent prayer of a righteous man availeth much. *(James 5:15-16, KJV)*

What we share with one another should go no further than prayer, and when we give it up to God, that should settle it. We should never become broadcasters of another's faults, shortcomings, or weaknesses, lest we want our own imperfections to be exposed by God. We should not be gossipers. We should walk worthy in the vocation where we are called as children of God and of the light.

Don't sow seeds of discord with your brethren! Don't do it within the body of Christ. Don't do it at home. Just don't do it! That's why we cannot and must not hold on to hurt of any kind. Neither should we walk in anything other than love.

Listen to this: hurt is still hurt no matter how you sum it up. If it you haven't emptied from your cup!

So don't hold on to the hurt! (The longer you hold on to it, the longer it will hold on to you!) Don't become its fatality. Be its victor through Christ Jesus! Don't stay in broken fellowship!

Been Broken

Certainly as I said previously, there are many ways to hurt as there are many kinds of hurt. One of those ways is through loss. No one likes to lose (in Greek, *apollumi*, which means to perish or lose or *zemioo*, which means to suffer loss) things. Whether it be a dearly loved one, a position (promotion) you have worked hard to get, loss of a job, repossession of a car, a house destroyed by flood, storm, or fire, eviction, foreclosure, or even our health, we find it hard to face loss. How does one bounce back from losing a spouse (whether by death, divorce, or separation), a close relative, your best friend, your children, or even the one you were espoused (engaged) to? How do we respond when the loss is by a sudden illness, incarceration for life, the senseless and selfishness of suicide, an unexpected and unexplained fatality, the horror of murder, or a tragic accident that has taken them away from our presence? Where does one find peace or consolation from the hurt? Would you even know to call on the God of all comfort?

What if it seems that your name and your good works have been tainted, slandered, or stained by horrible rumors or lies? How can one regain self-esteem when it seems your reputation is shot? Where does one draw the strength to go forward in the face of ridicule? What if society has labeled you a freak (a monstrosity because of a birth defect, illness, or deformity), or if by misfortune, you've succumbed to the cruelty, savagery, and inhumanity of rape (whether spiritually, emotionally, or physically), and it seems that you are on trial instead of the perpetrator? Maybe you have been diagnosed with full-blown AIDS virus or some other incurable disease. Given a short time to live, what would be your response or reaction? Consider this: God is our helper and deliverer!

> *God is our refuge and strength, an ever-present help in trouble. Psalm 46:1 KWSB – 1.1*

To defame is to injure or destroy the reputation by libel or slander, like defamation of character or character assignation. (This is what it means to soil someone).

If we want to guard our hearts, avoid having this type of behavior in our lives, and change the effects that hurt has on us, we are admonished to do these:

1. Shun (stay away from) the appearance of evil.

   But test and prove all things [until you can recognize] what is good: [to that] hold fast. Abstain from evil [shrink from it and keep aloof from it] in whatever form or whatever kind it may be. *(1 Thiess. 5:21-22, AMP)*

2. Don't let your good works be spoken evil of.

   Do not therefore let what seems good to you be considered an evil thing [by someone else]. [In other words, do not give occasion for others to criticize that which is justifiable for you]. [After all] the kingdom of God is not a matter of [getting the] food and drink [one likes], but instead it is righteousness (that state which makes a person acceptable to God) and [heart] peace and joy in the Holy Spirit. *(Rom. 14:16-17, AMP)*

3. Flee from youthful lust.

   Flee also youthful lusts: but follow righteousness, faith, charity, peace, with them that call on the Lord out of a pure heart. *(2 Tim. 2:22, KJV)*

4. Master evil with good and be honest!

   Recompense to no man evil; for evil. Provide things honest in the sight of all men. Be not overcome of evil, but overcome evil with good. *(Rom. 12:17, 21, KJV)*

5. We are not to use our liberty for our own foolish, lustful gain, though we have liberty (freedom) in Christ Jesus.

   For you, brethren, were [indeed] called to freedom: only [do not let your] freedom be an incentive to your flesh and an opportunity or excuse [for selfishness], but through love you should serve one another. *(Gal. 5:13, AMP)*

6. Be sober and watchful (alert)!

   Be sober, be vigilant, because your adversary the devil, as a roaming lion, walketh about, seeking whom he may devour. *(1 Pet. 5:8, KJV)*

   Let us fix our eyes on Jesus, the author and perfecter of our faith, who for the joy set before him endured the cross, scorning the shame, and sat down at the *right hand* of the throne of God. *(Heb. 12:2 KWSB; italics added)*

7. Keep our hearts and minds pure!

   He who has clean hands and a pure heart, who has not lifted himself up to falsehood or to what is false, nor sworn deceitfully. *(Ps. 24:4, AMP)*

   Blessed are the pure in heart: for they shall see God. *(Matt. 5:8, KJV)*

   Be perfect, be of good comfort, be of one mind, live in peace: and the God of love and peace shall be with you. *(2 Cor. 13:11, KJV)*

   And the peace of God, which passeth all understanding shall keep your hearts and minds through Christ Jesus. *(Phil. 4:7, KJV)*

In light of these aforementioned scenarios and godly remedies (solutions), ask yourself these questions:

Would you throw up your hands? Would you be willing and ready to throw in the towel, so to speak? Would you be ready to give up? Would your approach or outlook be one of self-preservation? Would your survival instinct take over, or would you concede that all hope was lost and there is no real reason to live? Are you willing to turn things over to God?

Let's take a brief moment and look at loss (we'll discuss it even further in a later chapter):

Loss for most of us is hard to accept—loss of trust, loss of hope, loss of innocence, loss of morality, to say the least. Some will even give up all hope because they undergo the loss of material possession. Sometimes we tend to lose ourselves in the void (emptiness, destitution,) of loss (in Hebrew, *abed'ah*, which means that which was lost). Loss, if given into could possibly annihilate us (in Greek, *apollumi* or to destroy fully).

> **Void** *1: containing nothing: EMPTY 2: being without something specified: devoid - blank, destitute, bereft*
>
> **Empty** *lacking value, force, sense or purpose: Futile, pointless, worthless, senseless - 1.2*

Remember Job? When dealing with his loss, he said, "Naked came I out of my mother's womb, and naked shall I return thither: the Lord gave, and the Lord hath taken away: blessed be the name of the Lord [This means that we are born without having any possessions and we certainly do not take anything with us when we die. Have you ever seen a U-Haul following a hearse to a burial? I know I haven't.]" *(Job 14:21, KJV)*

Ever try to turn to your peers only to have them shun you? Then by society, you appear hated because of ignorance. It even seems the medical field, certain experts treat you as a leper. It appears like you can't find comfort anywhere. Sinking deeper into despair, without a cure, without hope, and without a prayer, you might ask, "What am I to do?" Perhaps you wonder where you can go or to whom you can turn to when you're hurt so deeply. Do you break the silence or hold it in? Do you drown in self-pity or get on with living?

Jesus told us to look up (to Him) for our rescue, fulfillment, recovery, and saving when we began to see trouble come upon the earth:

> "There will be signs in the sun, moon and stars. On earth, nations will be in anguish and perplexity at the roaring and tossing of the sea. Men will faint from terror, apprehensive of what is coming on the world, for the heavenly bodies will be shaken... When these things begin to take place, *stand up* and *lift up* your heads, because your redemption is *drawing near.*"
> (Luke 21:25-26, 28, KWSB; italics added)

Don't get overwhelmed or feel there is no way out. Don't become baffled or bewildered. Don't let it cause you to sin. If you do not know the answer or cannot find your way, turn to Jesus. Get in the Word of God! Jesus said, "Search the scriptures; for in them ye think ye have eternal life: and they are they which testify of me" *(John 5:39, KJV)*

Therefore I say to you, though it seems you are left shattered and destitute, look up to Jesus and live!

What Are You to Do?

In Isaiah 53:3-5, we see that Christ Jesus took upon himself all our hurts in order to fill every void and bring us healing for every area of life. He tells us in John 10:10 (KJV), "The thief cometh not, but to steal, and to kill, and to destroy: I am come that they might have life; and that they might have it more abundantly."

And it is through Christ's love and life that we can live abundantly.

Through His love, we can be restored and renewed, finding strength and hope to move forward beyond our hurt or loss. You can "cast all your cares [hurts, woes, whatsoever is weighing you down] on Christ for he cares for you" *(1 Pet. 5:7, NKJV)*. Apostle Peter admonishes us also to "humble ourselves, that in due time God may exalt you. Be sober and vigilant because of our adversary the devil seeks to devour us. Resist the devil in faith knowing that the same identical sufferings are appointed throughout the body of Christ. That after we have suffered; God in all grace, Himself complete and make you what you ought to be, establish and ground you securely, and strengthen; and settle you" *(1 Pet 5:6-10 SPIB)*.

What a blessing!

We too much like the woman *(Luke 8:42-48)* with the issue of blood for those twelve long agonizing and painful years can turn to Jesus. Turn to the One who bore all our sickness, iniquities, and diseases in his own body, the One who nailed them all to the cross, being *the* Chief Sacrifice given once and for all. None other did that for us. None. Not Buddha, not Muhammad, not any other deity, not Martin Luther King Jr., no martyrs, none of the kings and their kingdoms, none of our forefathers, not even President Barack Obama. None, but Jesus Christ, Son of the Living God!

In this country and around the world, many look to our former president (Barack Obama) as though he would come in and save the day in an instant. They look to him as though he were a superhero. They try to paint him as a miracle worker who would get the country from under all its ills overnight. Then when things didn't go their way, they began cursing him, challenging him, ridiculing him, and questioning his authority, much like the Pharisees, Sadducees, scribes, and such of Jesus' day. They chose to look to man rather than to God the Father, who made them and is willing and able to help, heal, and restore them. Romans 1:25 (KJV) says, "Who changed the truth of God into a lie, and worshipped and served the creature rather than the Creator, who is blessed forever. Amen" We cannot save ourselves, though some try to portray it that way. Only Christ Jesus can save, deliver, and set us free.

Reach out and touch Him now as he's passing by. Invite Him into your heart and allow him to abide within.

Changing Our Mind-Set

There is this treacherous sort of an irony in our society (our land) today called the "I don't care" syndrome, and unfortunately, many people, especially our youth, have this diabolical way of thinking: with no regard whatsoever for others. It appears it's every man for himself, so to speak. It's about me, myself, and I. Few regard life as a blessing or a precious gift. There is no respect for elders, authority, or any other person other than self. Yet this generation surely wants to be respected. There is the usage of phrases such as, "I ain't no punk," "I'm not going to let you punk me out" or "I've got to do you before you can do me." Recklessly they try to prove their point, even at the endangerment of themselves and others. Not realizing it is Satan who has them already punked out, plucked up, sifted, and ready to be burned with fire. They are not prepared for heaven, are unfit to live and not ready to die. It is because we have become an amoral people without morals, without honesty, without self-control, without love, without God. What a cataclysmic disconnect in our society today!

This is what Jesus said would happen in Matthew 24:12, (KJV; italics added) "And because *iniquity* shall abound, the love of many shall wax cold"

Iniquity means to display evil (wicked) thoughts, traits, and behavior.

Here's a fact that is staggeringly alarming: there is this disregard for God! There is no regard for the true and living God, and none for mankind either. We see this disregard mentioned in scripture: "The [empty-headed] fool has said in his heart, There is no God. They are corrupt, they have done abominable deeds; there is none that does good or right" *(Ps. 14:1, KJV)*.

Maybe it is because we have the audacity or misconception that we will never have to answer to God (it seems to elude most) for every deed that's done in the body, action, or word spoken in this life. This attitude is simply shocking. Why do so many take God for granted? Seems there's no room or time for God or man. It is the approach or stance we should never take at any given time. And then there are those who say, "I got to get them before they get me!" It appears we have taken on the mind of Cain, as we see in Genesis 4:9 (KJV), "Am I my brother's keeper?" What a horrible shame if we only seem to care for ourselves, what's ours, and no more. Not caring about those we may pass by, ignoring, stepping on or beating them down to get what we want is a very tragic and destructive way to live. We must change our mind-set!

My friend, this is a trick of the devil! I praise God that He would not have us ignorant. Know that this is sin's inheritance to keep us from perfecting (growing up, maturing) and reaping God's most precious riches: His wisdom, knowledge, and truth; to keep us from benefiting from God's amazing grace; to keep us from seeing, experiencing, and understanding God's tender mercies and loving kindness for us; to keep us from ever knowing His love and sweet fellowship (the love of the Father for his Son, their love for us, and communion with his Holy Spirit); and to keep us from being one as Jesus and

> *"...Holy father, keep through thine own name those whom thou has given me, that they may be one, as we are. Jn 17:21 KJV — 1.3*

the Father are one. Also, it is to keep us from receiving eternal life, which is the gift of God for us all. The devil does not want us to know that sin carries a heavy price tag: death! And we should know that none of us are worthy, able, or even truly willing to pay for our sins.

> For the wages of sin is death; but the gift of God is eternal life
> through Jesus Christ our Lord. *(Rom. 6:23, KJV)*

It is our enemy's task to keep us from obeying, submitting, humbly seeking, and loving the Lord God. Satan has blinded, beguiled, schemed, connived, and cheated from the beginning. He tries to keep us bound, entangled, and off-center by shining the trappings of sin to entice us. But it is not the True Light, the Lord Christ Jesus. Satan's ultimate goal is to keep us perpetually backsliding as much as possible. He heightens his tactics so much so as to ensure that we also share his predestined fate: cut off forever from God! Although our adversary, the devil, tries to keep us from reaping the blessing God has for us, in the end all who put their trust in the Lord will certainly overcome him. Though it seems like things are working against us, know that if God is for us, there is *none* that can be against us.

Remember that "all things work together for the good of them that love God, who are the called according to His purpose" *(Rom. 8:28, KJV)*. It may not look good, feel good, sound good, taste good, or even smell good, but know that it will always work out for our good through God.

God's plan is for us to prosper in every area of life regardless of what the enemy or our flesh tries to tell us. God has made provision for us to succeed and to do it well in Him:

> Eyes have not seen, nor ears heard, neither has it entered into
> the hearts of man, the things which God has prepared for them
> that love him. But God hath revealed them unto us by his Spirit:
> for the Spirit searcheth all things, yea, the deep things of God.
> *(1 Cor. 2:9-10, KJV)*

It is as simple as this: receive his gift of life!

Here is a constant reminder that we are living in the last days and that Jesus Christ's return is approaching swiftly: the hardening of hearts. Apostle Paul said that in perilous times children would be disobedient to parents, men would be lovers of themselves, gain-seekers, traitors, having no natural affection *(2 Tim. 3:1-7)*. When we are focused on self and self alone, there is no room for anyone else. When pleasing the self (flesh, our sinful nature) is first and foremost, then we become our own god.

> Having a form of godliness, but denying the power thereof: from
> such turn away. *(2 Tim. 3:5, KJV)*

This is idolatry. It is a terrible mistake on our part. This is where we neglect and omit the One who made us, the One who is also our Heavenly Father. He provides all things for us and redeemed us for His namesake through the life, death, burial, and resurrection of His Son, Jesus Christ. Ask yourself this question: whatever happened to us loving the Lord our God with all our heart, with all our soul, and with all our strength and to loving our neighbor as we do ourselves?

> *These are* **the 1ˢᵗ and** 2ⁿᵈ *commandments that Jesus came to fulfill* **and establish Malt, 22:37-40 - 1.4**

I know you have heard the statement "what goes around comes around." The Bible gives light to this statement in Galatians 6:7-8 (KJV), which says, "Be not deceived; God is not mocked: for whatsoever a man soweth, that shall he also reap. For he that soweth to his flesh shall reap of the flesh corruption; but he that soweth to the Spirit shall of the Spirit reap life everlasting."

We should be attentive of the way we treat one another. We should be attentive of our attitude and our behavior as we interact or come in contact with others on a daily basis. We should take heed of this passage so that we can be the recipients of its great blessing and not recipients of corruption: "Let us not be weary in well doing: for in due season we shall reap, if we faint not" *(Gal. 6:9, KJV)*. With these words of solace and encouragement, why do we act faint? Perchance it is that we truly do not trust God entirely. Either we are not willing to obey the Lord or don't believe his word is true.

The golden rule says, "Do unto others as you would have them do unto you." If you every went to Sunday school or knew someone who went to Sunday School, then you've probably heard of this rule. And it's a very good rule to live by! It simply is saying however we want, desire, expect, or long to be treated, even if others do not treat us that way or reciprocate, we should and are to convey it upon them. Refusing to follow this rule will take us to sealing our fate with God's wrath. This becomes true when we are constantly being judgmental and harshly critical of others, omitting and overlooking self.

Here is a true saying in the scripture that can help you with your perspective of things: "that as a man thinketh [perception] in his heart, so is he" *(Prov. 23:7, KJV)*.

> There are those who curse their fathers and do not bless their mothers; those who are pure in their own eyes and yet *are* not *cleansed* of their filth; those whose eyes are ever so haughty, whose glances are so disdainful; those whose teeth are swords and whose jaws are set with knives to devour the poor from the earth, the needy from among mankind. *(Prov. 30:1114, KWSB)*

This scripture shows us another reason why we should not be judgmental. We see how horrible it is to be a judgmental person. When we have a judgmental complex, we become self-righteous in our own eyes.

This particular passage refers to what the apostle addressed concerning godlessness in the last days. Paul proclaimed that people would become extremely irreverent, harsh, brutish even. How severely devastating it is to their own hurt and demise that they would oppose the truth. Therefore, when we think on these lines, we bring condemnation upon ourselves. This view or mentality is certainly running rampant in America today! It is even seen among many who profess to be Christians. The god of this world has blinded their eyes. The scriptures say,

> People will be *lovers of themselves*, lovers of money, boastful, proud, abusive, disobedient to their parents, ungrateful, unholy, *without love*, unforgiving, slanderous, *without self-control*, brutal, *not lovers of* the *good*, treacherous, rash, conceited, lovers of pleasure rather than lovers of God—having a form of godliness but denying its power. Have nothing to do with them. They are the kind who worm their way into houses and *gain control over* weak-willed women, who are loaded down with sins and are swayed by all kinds of *evil desires*, always learning but never able to acknowledge the truth. Just as Jannes and Jambres opposed Moses, so also these men oppose the truth—men of depraved minds, who as far as the faith is concerned, are rejected. But they will not get far because, as in the case of those men, their folly will be clear to everyone. *(2 Tim. 3:1-9, AMP; italics added)*

The Lord Jesus spoke about the condemnation we bring on ourselves when He declared that he came to save the world. His mission was not to bring condemnation to us, but life, freedom, redemption, love, joy, and peace. When we or if we reject His wonderful offering, then we have condemned ourselves already. Thus Jesus shared with us this truth about Himself, the Light that shines upon all who come into the world and the darkness that some try to cling to:

> For God sent not his Son into the world to condemn the world; but that the world through him might be saved. He that believeth on him is not condemned: but he that believeth not is condemned already, because he hath not believed in the name of the only begotten Son of God. And this is the condemnation, that light is come into the world, and men loved darkness rather than light, because their deeds were evil. For everyone that doeth evil hateth the light, neither cometh to the light, lest his deeds should be reproved. *(John 3:17-20, KJV)*

Whatever your perception is will be your outlook (perspective, standpoint, or point of view) on life, our view can become very tainted if we allow the cares of life, our past wounds, or our woes to overtake us. Having wrong and evil motives will also cause our vision or perception to be distorted.

If we want our view to change, we must change our outlook!

CHAPTER 2

WHY SO JUDGMENTAL?

From a Bird's-Eye View

We sometimes, presumably unaware, go about passing on sentences to those around us. Jesus taught us in Matthew 5:9—11 volumes concerning our aptitude and attitude in our response to being taunted, rejected, treated unfairly, or judged. Verses 43—48 instruct us on how to love those who do not love us.

Look at what Jesus says about loving our enemies: "love your enemies, bless those who curse you, do good unto them and pray for those which despitefully use and persecute [torment] you" *(Matt. 5:44, NKJV-SSB).*

Often we are quick to cut others down with our words when we feel that they are wrong. We can be swift to judge, but instead we should be slow to anger, swift to hear, and in most cases, slow to speak (James 1:19). We should take our cue from what Jesus said in Matthew 7:1—12. Verses 1—6 teach us to be careful how we view others, letting us know that we should not be faultfinders (always critical) of others, but rather we should examine ourselves first. This will keep us from being hypocritical and judgmental. If we apply verses 7-12 in actual daily living, we would truly experience a greater return. We would also encounter a clearer perspective of others.

Sometimes we can be all too critical of others. Jesus gave us checkpoints in Matthew 7:3-4 (KJV):

> "And why beholdest thou the mote that is in thy brother's eye, but considerest not the beam that is in thine own eye? Or how wilt thou say to thy brother, Let me pull out the mote [small particle, speck] out of thine eye: and behold, a beam is in thine own eye?"

It seems we rapidly move to give our unwarranted advice or opinion about someone else's faults, shortcomings, or handicaps and do not look at ourselves. We readily point the finger, not realizing that there are three fingers pointing back at us. We, like the old adage says, tend to "make a mountain out of a molehill." We don't seem to consider the feelings of others when we are miserable. We go about as if we seek to make them as miserable as we are, making truth of the statement "Misery loves company!" Just ask Job.

Jesus went on to say, "Thou hypocrite, first cast out the beam out of thine own eye: and then shalt thou see clearly to cast out the mote of thy brother's eye" *(Matt. 7:5, KJV)*.

When we cannot see clearly, we make the matter greater than it really is. We blow it out of proportion, act out preposterously, and give life and power to something that is or was powerless. We do so all because our vision is impaired by our outlook due to the things we are unwilling to shed, haven't given up, and won't let go or rid ourselves of. It is just like these words that say "the pot calling the kettle black," which is when someone accuses another of a fault they are also guilty of. They don't realize that they are the same but in different degrees; (in the same boat or made from the same metal, in a matter of speaking).

I want to admonish you with this: if your vision is impaired, come this moment and allow (ask) Jesus to anoint your eyes with eye salve so you can regain your sight and be healed! *(John 9:6-11, Rev. 3:18)*.

Many times we do not realize the power of our tongue and the deadly poison that can strike as it assails, ignorantly striking without any remorse, without any thought of the aftershock or repercussion that might occur from its fatal blow. Here's a bit of wisdom for you:

> *Psalm 52:2-5 speaks about the power & devastation of the tongue. Here It describes how vile & full of devilish mischief "it" (the tongue) is. - 1.5*

> The mouth of a righteous man is a well of life: but violence covereth the mouth of the wicked. Hatred stirreth up strife: but love covereth all sins. *(Prov. 10:11-12, KJV)*

> Death and life are in the power of the tongue: they that love it shall eat the fruit thereof. *(Prov. 18:21, KJV)*

Jesus called the Pharisees a generation of vipers because of the slanderous tongues they were so eager and swift to use against Him. He told us that we will know the tree by its fruit. In the later part of verse 34 in Matthew 12 (KJV), he said, "for out of the abundance of the heart the mouth speaketh."

It is like the saying "You are what you eat" (you are what you feed upon). Whatever is in you, that's what going to inevitably come out of you. If it is bitterness, resentment, jealousy, hatred, envy, strife, or the like, then that's what will come out when you speak. If it is love, joy, peace, goodness, gentleness, mercy, then that's what your words will be: full of life!

In other words if you love life, you will speak words of life and/or positivity and reap that. If you speak words of death or negativity all the time, that's what you are going to reap. We can declare poverty or lack over our lives with our own mouths. This brings us to the law of reciprocity (sowing and reaping), which I spoke of earlier:

> Be not deceived; God is not mocked: for whatsoever a man soweth, that shall he also reap. For he that soweth to his flesh shall of the flesh reap corruption; but he that soweth to the Spirit shall of the Spirit reap life everlasting. And let us not be weary in well doing: for in due season we shall reap, if we faint not. *(Gal. 6:7-9,* KJV)

If we use our tongue to cut others down or up, then we are sowing or speaking death. When we love life, we will bless and not curse. We will speak of peace and not of strife. Most often when we lash out at others, it is because we are hurting or have not gotten over past hurts. And if we are still harboring ill feelings, we must release them to the Lord for this should not be evident in the life of the believer.

We can get a good look at this in James 3:1-12 (KWSB), where the apostle admonished us about the tongue and its attributes. In verses 1-4 (italics added) it says, "If we are never *at fault* in *what* we *say* we are perfect; able to keep our whole body *in check*, just as we put bits in horses mouths that they *may obey* us, then we can turn the whole body." Verses 5-8 speak of the tongue being "a small part of the body, it corrupts the whole person, set on fire by hell, no man can tame it, restless evil; and full of deadly poison." And verses 9—12 state that "with it we praise the Lord and Father and with it curse men, who God made in his likeness, it shouldn't be, fresh and salt water doesn't flow from the same spring; and neither can a fig tree bear olives, or a grapevine figs."

It truly takes the loving guidance of God the Father through the Holy Spirit to help us with the tongue, which can at times seem to flow with honey and at other times flow with deadly poison like an asp or viper. Only God can tame the tongue. And without the Lord (Adonai) God's help, then we with this little member will destroy love, hope, and peace and bring hurt to ourselves and others.

Where Has the Love Gone?

Have we as a people forgotten so soon about the God of love and that God is love for you, for me, and for the whole world? He is love to redeem and reconcile us back to Himself. He gave us his only begotten Son; Jesus died! It wasn't Aunt Betsy, Uncle Bob, Pastor Feelings, Prophet Told-You-So, etc., not the twelve apostles, none of the great martyrs before us, none of these but the Lord Jesus Christ. He died laying down His life for his sheep and becoming the supreme sacrifice once and for us all. He did it through the shedding His own blood as the Lamb of offering. Hanging upon that cross, Jesus took our place that all might come unto repentance and that none of us should perish. He died that all who would receive him could have everlasting life.

Merriam-Webster defines *perish* this way: to become destroyed or ruined. This especially means to have one's life come to an end or to die, expire. It is denoted in scripture as to be lost, cut off, destroyed, without hope, or unredeemed.

The movie *What's Love Got to Do with It* was about Tina Turner's life story. It depicted how she came to be a pop star. It showed all she endured for the sake of loving someone she believed loved her, only to find out it wasn't equally shared. Tina found that although someone says they love you, that's not always what they convey. Ike's (her husband's) actions exemplified the actions of a very selfish, self-centered, belligerent, arrogant, and angry person.

If he could not have his way, he'd display violent, degrading, and hurtful behavior. His ways were deplorable. He threw erratic outbursts of temper and afterward turned around to show—or rather, buy—Tina's love. He threw money at the problem, which never fixed it. Money answers a lot of things, but it never answers the need to be respected, nurtured, and loved. Her own mother was entrapped, ensnared, and blinded by things he would give, which she seemed to value more than her daughter's happiness and welfare. You can't buy love!

Out of Ike's brokenness and insecurities, he turned on the one person who truly cared for him. He stripped her of dignity, derobed her of pride, self esteem, and self-worth. His love was for himself (full of usury, to get all you can and can all you get) and not for the woman he claimed he loved. He treated her as though the world revolved around him and him only. His love was toxic, polluted, and tainted. Tina suffered because of the hurt he desperately needed to be healed and delivered from. Ike didn't know that the husband was to love his wife as himself for a man in his right mind would not inflict hurt, pain, and anguish upon himself. He did not know and could not love her as Christ loved the church and gave himself for it because he wasn't in relationship with the Lord of heaven. Ike hadn't experienced the depth of the love of Christ; thus he couldn't show it in his actions, words, or deeds. He, like so many of us, hadn't come to grips or terms with what love really is.

So many of us often use the words "I love you" loosely. We'll say it knowing that that's not what we have within our hearts. Jesus spoke about loving only those who say they love us, but He urged us to love even our enemies. It's a hard saying, you might think. This can only be done when the unconditional love of God manifests in our lives. It becomes more than something we say but also something we do. We can find what unconditional love is and its attributes in 1 Corinthians 13. Love's persona should implement these features when we are endowed with God's love: it endures (suffers) long, is kind, does not envy or boil with jealousy, isn't puffed up (haughty), isn't boastful, conceited (arrogant or inflated with pride), isn't rude, doesn't act unbecomingly, isn't easily provoked or self-seeking, thinks no evil, and doesn't rejoice at injustice or unrighteousness. Instead it rejoices in truth, bears all things, believes all things, hopes in all things, and endures all things. Love never fails.

This love should be evident in our walk with others. It should be a viable part of our characteristic as believers. In John 15:13 (KJV), Jesus said, "Greater love hath no man than this, that a man lays down his life for his friends." These are true words to live by. Here the

Lord gives us the prime example of true love for our fellow men. This was also demonstrated in the relationship of David and Jonathan (King Saul's son) in 1 Samuel 18-20. We have a witness of this recorded in the Old and New Testament.

How many of you would be willing to give your life for your friends?

Instead of being loving, kind, and considerate, do we, like him (Ike), behave badly with others? Are we portraying to others that we love them or ourselves when we really don't? If we don't love ourselves, we surely cannot love or are incapable of loving anyone else. We will not be able to exemplify Christ in our actions, words, or deeds. This is when we act as if someone owes us immensely. We do so without regard for those who we are affecting with our toxicity. It is because we are hurting that we don't know how to love and are not sufficiently equipped to love others. Instead of having healthy relationships, we end up with toxic ones, and they are toxic because of our unresolved issues. We'll land there if we won't and don't turn it over completely to the Lord Jesus.

Like Tina, I had my share of toxic relationships, toxic because they were detrimental to my well-being (spirit, soul, and body), toxic because they were degrading, defaming, slanderous, vicious, cruel, and at times violent, toxic because they were at the hands of those who I thought cared for me and those I trusted. Perhaps I was stricken by such things because I hadn't truly dealt with rejection, disappointments, past hurts, and the like. Like many of you, I pushed or shoved those things back to the far recesses of my mind. Before I could fully recover, I found myself in another relationship that ended in a breakup, wrecked!

When I cried out (repented), God heard me, healed me, and taught me to forgive and love again. God's agape love reached me where I was. Although I was out of place, out of position, and out of right fellowship with God, He was still vested in my life. Thanks be unto God. He still redeems, restores, and sets us free! The Lord mended my brokenness! He filled in the gaps (the void). I also thank God for my early teaching in His word and about prayer. Prayer does change things!

This unconditional love was demonstrated through the covenanted relationship of David and Jonathan. Here we are shown the depth of love greater than that which is transcended through brotherly love (*philios*), maternal love (*storge*), or love between a man and a woman (*eros*); it is agape, God's divine love. It is the love of Christ that passes (supersedes, goes beyond) all knowledge that will fill us with "all the fullness of God." It is love unconditional. This love has no boundaries and is limitless. If we could measure God's love, it would register more vast in depth, width, length, height, and breadth than any other love. This love is immeasurable because of its greatness. It is almost indescribable.

> [17]*That Christ may dwell* in *your* hearts *by faith; that ye, being rooted* and *grounded* in love. [18]*May be able to comprehend* with all *saints what is the breadth, and length and depth, and height;* [19]And to *know the love* of Christ, which *passeth* all *knowledge, that ye might be filled with* all the *fullness of God. KJV - 1.6*

David and Jonathan's relationship was based on covenant. In this covenant, all that David had was Jonathan's, and all that Jonathan had belonged to David. They interchanged wardrobe, lifestyles, friendship, and love. Their lives were full of each other. No harm could be befall either of them for they looked out for each other. They were not homosexuals. Nor did they have unnatural tendencies. They were real men who knew how to love beyond themselves, beyond their needs, desires, or wants. They loved unselfishly. This was the same love God bestowed (presented, gave) upon us in John 3:16 through the sacrifice of his Son, Jesus Christ, our Savior.

God wants our lives to be full!

> For God so loved the world, that he gave his only begotten Son, that whosoever believes in him, should not perish, but have everlasting life. *(John 3:16, KJV)*

God wants to fill our lives with His fullness. We can only receive this if we have been or are willing to be transformed in heart, mind, and will (soul). Also, if we submit or subject ourselves to the tender molding of His mighty hands, here's what the Holy Spirit says we must do:

How can we change our mind-set, outlook, and perception?

The word of God has our answer:

1. We must walk in love.

> Therefire be imitators of God [copy Him and follow His example], as well-beloved children [imitate their father] And walk in love, [esteeming and delighting in one another] as Christ loved us and gave Himself up for us, a slain offering and sacrifice to God [for you, so that it became] a sweet fragrance. *(Eph. 5:1-2 AMP)*

> For, brethren, ye have been called unto liberty: only use not liberty for an occasion to the flesh, but by love serve one another. For all the law is fulfilled in one word, even in this: Thou shalt love thy neighbor as thyself. But if ye bite and devour one another, take heed that ye be not consumed one of another. This I say then, Walk in the Spirit, and ye shall not fulfill the lust of the flesh. *(Gal. 5:13-16, KJV)*

2. We must keep our minds and trust centered on the Lord.

> You will guard him *and* keep him in perfect *and* constant peace whose mind [both its inclination and its character] is stayed on You, because he commits himself to You, leans on You, *and* hopes confidently in You. So trust in the Lord (commit yourself to Him, lean on Him, hope confidently in Him) forever; for the Lord God is an everlasting Rock [the Rock of Ages]. *(Isa. 26:3-4, AMP)*

3. We must surrender our mind, will, and intellect to the knowledge of God.

    [Inasmuch as we] refute arguments and theories and reasonings and every proud and lofty thing that sets itself up against the [true] knowledge of God; and we lead every thought and purpose away captive into obedience of Christ (the Messiah, the Anointed One). *(2 Cor. 10:5, AMP)*

4. We must put on the mind of Christ.

    Let this same attitude and purpose and [humble] mind be in you which was in Christ Jesus; [Let Him be your example in humility:] *(Phil. 2:5, AMP)*

5. We must become a living sacrifice daily and renew our minds.

    I APPEAL to you therefore, brethren, and beg of you to view of [all] the mercies of God, to make a decisive dedication of your bodies [presenting all your members and faculties] as a living sacrifice, holy (devoted, consecrated) and well pleasing to God, which is your reasonable (rational, intelligent) service and spiritual worship. Do not be conformed to this world (this age), [fashioned after and adopted to its external, superficial customs]; but be transformed (changed) by the [entire] renewal of your mind [by its new ideals and its new attitude], so that you may prove [for yourselves] what is the good and acceptable and perfect will of God, even the thing which is good and acceptable and perfect [in His sight for you]. *(Rom. 12:1-2, AMP)*

6. We must put on the whole armor of God.

    Put on the full armor of God so that you can stand against the devil's schemes. For our struggle is not against flesh and blood, but against the rulers, against the authorities, against the *powers of* this dark *world* and against the spiritual forces of evil in the heavenly realms. Therefore *put on* the full armor of God, so that when the day of evil comes, you may be able to *stand your ground*, and after you have done everything, to stand. *Stand firm* then, with the belt of truth buckled around your waist, with the breastplate of righteousness in place, and with your feet fitted with the readiness that comes from the gospel of peace. In addition to all this, take up the shield of faith, with which you can extinguish all the flaming arrows of the *evil one*. Take the helmet of salvation and the sword of the Spirit, which is the word of God. And pray in the Spirit on all occasions with all kind of prayers and requests. With this in mind, be alert and always keep on praying for all saints. *(Eph. 6:11-18, KWSB; italics added)*

7. Think on these things.

And the peace of God, which passeth all understanding, shall keep your hearts and minds through Christ Jesus. Finally, brethren, whatsoever things are true, whatsoever things are honest, whatsoever things are just, whatsoever things are pure, whatsoever things are lovely, whatsoever things are of good report; if there be any virtue, if there be any praise, think on these things. *(Phil. 4:7-8, KJV)*

He Picks Up the Pieces

I am so glad that Christ came and took away all pain, sorrow, and grief. For this cause, it was written in Isaiah 53:3--5 (KJV),

He is despised and rejected of men; a man of sorrows, and acquainted with grief: and we hid as it were our faces from him; he was despised, and we esteemed him not. Surely he hath borne our griefs, and carried our sorrows: yet we did esteem him stricken, smitten of God, and afflicted. But he was wounded for our transgressions; he was bruised for our iniquities: the chastisement of our peace was upon him; and with his stripes we are healed.

Christ was betrayed, battered, and beaten beyond recognition, thrashed within inches of his life, flogged so you and I could be restored, reconciled to our rightful place with God. He was scourged for the sins of the whole world. His body was torn and shredded by the cat-o'-nine-tails (the ends of each lash had pieces of broken bones, stone, and metal tied into it). Thirty-nine stripes they laid upon him. His beard was ripped by the handfuls from his face. He was bludgeoned and lashed so badly, he was hardly recognizable. He was bruised, black and blue all over, spat upon and slapped brutally for our redemption. He was crowned with thorns that were plaited together then shoved hard into his skull. (All these things transpired before He ever took up the cross). Then they led Jesus up Golgotha's (the skull's) hill carrying his cross. Up a hill called Calvary where he was crucified (nailed) on that cross (nine-inch spikes in his hand, a twelve-inch spike through his feet) he had to bear.

He suffered the pain of rejection for us. He cried out to the Father at the sixth hour (noon) with a loud voice, saying, "Eli, Eli, lama sabachthani?" which means, "My God, my God, why hast thou forsaken me?" He suffered the shame. He alone suffered the anguish of the weight of the sins of the world. He suffered for you and for me, and after suffering there (pushing himself up ever so often for air, perhaps), at the ninth hour (three o'clock) Jesus cried, "It is finished" (He accomplished it all), gave up the ghost, and died; they pierced his side.

It was a bloody, gruesome, horrific scene from the garden, to the judgment hall, to the cross, yet he was humble and obedient even to his death on the cross *(Luke 22:44; Phil. 2:8)*. The price of redemption was paid. Early in the morning, the third day (on the first day of the week) after being in the grave for two days and two nights, Christ arose from the grave! He arose with all power in his hands, power over death (the curse sin brought on us), hell, and the grave!

> And Jesus came and spoke unto them, saying; All power is given
> unto me in heaven and in earth. *(Matt. 28:18, KJV)*

In Revelation 1:18 (KJV), Jesus said, "I am he that liveth, and was dead; and behold, I am alive forevermore. Amen; and have the keys of hell and of death."

> But now that you have been set free from sin and have become the
> slaves of God, the benefit you reap leads to holiness, and the result
> is eternal life. For the wages of sin is death, but the gift of God is
> eternal life in Christ Jesus our Lord. *(Rom. 6:22-23, KWSB)*

This was the work of redemption. This was the new covenant written between God and man written with the blood of His Son, Jesus Christ, the Lamb of Sacrifice. All this so we might be freed from sin, death, the grave, and hell and have a right to eternal life with Him. All this just to reconcile us back to God and place (restore) us in our rightful position with the Father.

> Without the shedding of blood there can be no remission [taking
> away, wiping out] of sin. *(Heb. 9:22, SPLB)*

Christ Jesus took our place so we would not have to die for our sins. He bore the full brunt of the sentence for sin's awful penalty so that you and I could go free. We are no longer sin's captives; we're saved by grace through faith. No more working for sin's wages, death; now we can receive the gift of God—eternal life. We are no longer children of darkness; now we are children of His Light. We are no longer bastards; now we, through His love, are made sons of God. No more sheep scattered without a shepherd; now He is our Savior, and we are His very own. It is through the love of the Father that Jesus came, lived, suffered, died, was buried, and arose again so that He alone could

> *And the vessel that he made of clay was marred in the hand of the potter; and he made it again another vessel, as seemed good to the potter to make it. Jer. 18:4 - 1.8*

mend, heal, and make whole again all our lives. God the Potter took the broken pieces of our shattered, dashed, decimated lives and made us into new vessels for his glory.

Hallelujah! Whatever you do, don't get stuck, and if you get stuck, don't stay stuck with your back against the wall!

Back Against the Wall

Back against the wall, no place, no space
can you find to crawl or to slide
Out of the situation that oppress you, pin you down
Back against the wall, obscure skies surround
everything you do, you reach, you touch
Can't seem to get a grip, still sinking
further with every clutch
Back against the wall, the dismal height, you're
pivoting in unseen woe, assailing you
Every insult impaling against the wall
No, you're not standing tall, crumbling,
crumbling, crumbling
It seems that with each moment you
fall back against the wall
Unable to breathe or take one breath in, seems
your circumstances has withdrawn your wind
It's hard to cry. you feel you're left, forsaken to
die, left alone hanging back against the wall
Back against the wall, wanting to exhale, it
seems you a deeper and deeper impaled
Trapped from without and within, can't get free,
your tongue to the roof of your mouth does cleave
Though it seems you're stuck betwixt a rock
and a hard place, no refuge can you find
Though you've cried out for solace and desired
peace to be restored to your mind
Hanging hopelessly in the unending
darkness without a friend to lean on
No one has noticed, seems no one cares that
you are stuck, pinned back against the wall
The mistakes that you've made threw you into
this pit, unaware of danger lingering there
Though at this moment your desire is to quit
while you're nailed back against the wall

Though now it seems you're left trembling,
thinking how you're surpressed by the chaos
Feeling the chill from it all, standing in
total duress, distressed, out on a limb
The thread you're holding keeps dwindling down
Engulfed in the mess as life's guillotine your head sits on
Like a rubber band over wound as you
dangle it seems back against the wall
Don't give up, don't lose hope, and don't give
in; look up and live; you still can win
Look and see that your redemption draweth
nigh; reach out for your destiny to succeed
Despite the fact that at this hour
you're back against the wall

So today, receive your healing in the name of Jesus!

CHAPTER 3

WHY? (WHY WE HURT)

Hurt will make you question whether you are on the right path, whether you are going in the right direction, or whether you're doing the right thing. Hurt can cause you to second-guess yourself. It can obscure your judgment and blindside you. Hurt will cause you not to know which way is up (lose all sense of direction). It can cause you to question whether you're coming or going. Sometimes hurt will cause you to reexamine and to reflect on life (to question why you're here, why you were ever born, what the purpose or meaning of your life is, even why this is happening to you). It will cause you to look hard upon past mistakes, present moves, and future decisions. Hurt done to you by others can cause you to lower your standards (morally, ethically, and spiritually).

Hurt, be it from domestic violence or a broken heart, can also cause you to fall into one toxic relationship after another. Before long you are the one lashing out and causing others hurt because hurt people hurt people! True statement!

Hurt can cause you to become oppressed (crushed) or depressed (saddened or discouraged). Depression or oppression can have a crippling effect of hurt if it is not released from our lives. Depression is one of the major causes of suicide and the increase of suicide among young adults and teens. Depression may seem like you've lost your confidence and grown a bit indecisive. With your outlook now clouded by fears, you may become afraid, apprehensive to take a chance, afraid you will be hurt again, afraid to be let down, to face one more disappointment, one more heartbreak, one more failure, or one more defeat, yet nothing beats a failure but a try.

Here's what the Bible says about falling down and getting back up again:

> A just man falls down 7 times and gets up again. *(Prov. 24:16, SPLB)*

> Many evils confront the [consistently] righteous, but the Lord delivers him out of them all. *(Ps. 34:19, AMP)*

> The steps of a [good] man are directed and established by the Lord when He delights in his way [and He busies Himself with his every step]. Though he falls, he shall not be utterly cast down; for the Lord grasps his hand in support and upholds him. *(Ps. 37:23-24, AMP)*

Though we fall down or are knocked down by circumstances or situations, we don't have to stay down. We don't have to wallow in self-pity. We can get back up again!

> **Just:** *upright, right righteous, moral, decent, honest, virtuous* — 2.1

For some of us, we hurt because of misuse, whether verbal (defamation, vilification, disdain, slander, character assassination), emotional (rejected love), or physical (abuse, molestation, unlawful sexual activity, assault, prostitution, pornography), neglect, abandonment, or even the travesty of murder. It seems no one likes to admit when they hurt or are hurting. We tend to keep silent. We attempt to conceal it and try to hide it. Blinded, it seems we become overthrown with it; our behavior changes because of it. Our bodies gives in to it; our faces are overcast by it. We can become indifferent, cold, and callous. Hurt left untreated soon turns to bitterness, and bitterness to hatred (unresolved anger). Left ensnared in this state, unchanged and unaltered, one could become self-inflicting and self-destructive. We see and read the effects of this type of behavior in the news. When left unchecked and out of balance, it leaves a great path of devastation. From anger to pent-up aggression to vengeance, a very toxic and explosive place to be. Here are some facts:

> Offense: 2 the act of attacking: ATTACK, ASSAULT 4b the state of being insulted or morally outraged 5 a breach of moral or social code: SIN. Offend: to cause discomfort or pain: HURT. *(Merriam-Webster's Dictionary and Thesaurus)*

During the 1994 Back-to-the-Bible 2 Conference with Bishop T. D. Jakes in Charleston, West Virginia, Dr. Mark Hanby spoke these words which are evident and true: "Stay out the house of offense so you won't be on the defense."

In Romans 12:19 and Hebrews 10:30, the Lord declares, "Vengeance is mine, I will repay!" It is not ours to exact or to dish out. No matter how hurt, overwrought, insulted (offended), or disturbed we may be, we are not to move from anger to vengeance or vindication. We are not to respond as though we are magistrate, juror, and executioner.

The Bible says to render not evil for evil.

> Do not let yourself be *overcome* [overtaken, consumed] by evil, but *overcome* [master] evil with good. *(Rom. 12:21, AMP; italics added)*

Don't be so easily slighted or act as though you're always being rubbed the wrong way. Apostle Paul cautions us about being angry and allowing it to cause us to do wrong (to do evil, act out wickedly, sin):

> Be ye *angry*, and sin not: let not the sun go down upon your wrath: Neither give place to the devil *(Eph. 4:26-27, KJV; italics added)*

Vital and viable words to live (pattern ourselves) by!
We are instructed to live peaceably with all men, to be peacemakers.

> Blessed [enjoying enviable happiness, spiritually prosperous with life-joy and satisfaction in God's favor and salvation, regardless of their outward conditions] are the *makers* and *maintainers* of *peace*, for they shall be called the sons of God! *(Matt. 5:9, AMP; italics added)*

> Recompense to no man evil for evil. Provide things honest in the sight of all men. If it is possible, as much as lieth in you, *live peaceably* with all men. *(Rom. 12:17-18, KJV; italics added)*

> We are to *follow* [strive for] *peace* and *holiness* [consecration] with all men, *without* which we *cannot see* God. Looking diligently lest any man fail of the grace of God; lest any root of bitterness springing up trouble you, and thereby many be defiled; Lest there be any fornicator, or profane person, as Esau, who for one morsel of meat sold his birthright. For ye know how afterward, when he would have inherited the blessing, he was rejected: for he found no place no repentance, though he sought it carefully with tears. *(Heb. 12:14-17, KJV; italics added)*

If we do follow peace and holiness, we won't forfeit our birthright like Esau did. We will see God! We will be his beloved children! We will not forfeit that which Jesus gained back for us through his death on the cross and resurrection from the grave.

How to Suffer Long or Endure

In life, things will not always go smoothly. I have found out that when God chooses you as a vessel for His glory, it seems that you suffer long. This means you have to endure or go through hardships for an extended period of time. It is only the process of shaping, molding, and making of you: the vessel.

I have learned this: The greater the blessing, the greater the test. The greater the task, the greater the reward (satisfaction). The greater the call, the greater the reply (response). And the greater God uses you, the greater the adversary (the devil) comes against you.

We all have a period of testing, going through trials until we pass, just like in school. (If you learn the lesson, you can pass the test, so pass your tests!) It is only the trying of our faith! Sometimes it is as if we go through on a never-ending cycle. It will make you wonder if you will see the light of day or even get a break from the constant onslaught of the cares of life. That's when the "woe is me" syndrome can have a tendency to kick or creep in. You may then settle into a pity party, where you celebrate the honoree: yourself. You may find yourself saying things like, "Why is this happening to me? Why me? What did I do to deserve this?" The question is, Why not you? Cares come and go. We shouldn't be overcome(overwhelmed) by them.

> *Beloved, think it not strange concerning the fiery trial which is to try you, as though some strange thing happened unto you. I Peter 4:12 - 2.2*

Consider Job's plight and all he endured, all he lost, yet he worshipped God in the midst of his troubles. (We will discuss Job's loss in a later chapter.) King David in Psalms 34:15, 17-19, and 34:22 testified of God's eyes and ears being upon and open to the righteous. He tells how the Lord delivers them from all their troubles and afflictions and redeems those who trust Him. There's an old adage which says "If you live long enough, trouble will find you." Job said it this way: "Man that is born of a woman a few days, and full of trouble" *(Job 14:1, KJV)*. And that's this thing we call living. In 1 Peter 4:12, the apostle admonished us not to think it strange or become bewildered when we are faced with fiery trials. In other words, don't get crushed or displaced when you go through hard times! Don't whine about it, but go in and through it with confidence, victory, and peace. Know that we have a High Priest who has been touched on all points: Christ Jesus, the Living Bread! Jesus said it best in John 16:33, when He gave us a pledge to take comfort in him despite whatever befalls us in this world. No matter the trial, test, circumstance, or situation, He is our Champion! Glory to God! Through Christ Jesus we can overcome every trial!

> *These things I have spoken unto you, that in me ye might have peace. In this world ye shall have tribulation; but be of good cheer, I have overcome the world.* **John 16:33 — 2.3**

Hear the words of King Solomon in Ecclesiastes 9:11 (KJV).

> I returned, and saw under the sun, that the race is not to the swift, nor the battle to the STRONG, neither yet bread to the wise, nor yet riches to men of understanding, nor yet favour to men of skill; but time and chance happeneth to them all.

Solomon described certain constants and the equalizing variables: time and chance. He also stated in chapter 1:9 that there is nothing new under the sun. History does repeat itself! See that there is not no-thing new. Realize that all things in this life are on a cycle.

We see this daily through styles, fads, trends, etc. Though we go through trials or troubles, we must not faint but make it to the other side.

For example, in sports we see this quite often. It is not always the team that won the coin toss that necessarily wins the contest (game) but rather the one who was more vigilant, hungry, and thirsty for the win that comes out the victor. The victory goes to the one that has stuck it out, run on, and continues to the end. They could have been the underdog, so to speak, coming into it, but they leave with victory. They have outlasted or ousted their opponent.

Jesus made it clear when he said, "But he who endures to the end shall be saved" *(Matt. 24:13, AMP)*. (We talked about enduring earlier.) We are encouraged by the Lord not to give up, not to falter, not to wane in our faith or be deceived but rather to hold on despite what we face. If we abide and continue in Christ Jesus, we will surely make it to the end. He reassures us to trust in His saving power. Since we cannot depend on flesh, it is apparent we can only truly depend on God.

Look at what Romans 9:16 (AMP) says: "So then [God's gift] is not a question of human will and human effort, but of God's mercy. [It depends not on one's own willingness or on his strenuous exertion as in running a race, but on God's having mercy on him.]" This lets us know that it is not about what power or authority we have, neither in what we think we can do. That is why Apostle Paul was able to declare in Philippians 4:13 (KJV), "I can do all things through Christ which strengthens me."

> Jesus said, "I am the vine, ye are the branches: He that abideth in me, and I in him, the same bringeth forth much fruit: for without me ye can do nothing." *(John 15:5, KJV)*

These passages of scripture shows us that we cannot trust in flesh (humanity) or what we can do but that we can trust completely in God to bring us through every trial and test victoriously. In Zechariah 4:6 (AMP), the prophet said it like this:

> Then he said to me, This [addition of the bowl to the candlestick, causing it to yield a ceaseless supply of oil from the olive trees] is the word of the Lord to Zerubbabel, saying, Not by might, nor by power, but by My Spirit [of Whom the oil is a symbol], says the Lord of hosts.

Here the Lord assures us that His Spirit will flow out upon us like a never-ending supply of oil when we rely on (tap into) Him and His word. We are also warned not to put all our trust in flesh or our own minds but to trust God completely and commit our ways (gifts, talents, lifestyles), heart (thoughts, intents), understanding (mind, intellect), and lives (spirit, soul, and body) to him in Psalm 37:3-9 and Proverbs 3:5-8.

What Is Abuse?

As mentioned above, abuse can be identified in many forms, whether spiritual, verbal, physical, whether through molestation, torment, entrapment, torture, a ravaging illness that has no cure, or harassment of any type. It is something that can be called a disease.

Disease is defined this way:

> A disordered or incorrectly functioning organ, part, structure, or system of the body resulting from the effect of genetic or developmental errors, infection, poisons, nutritional deficiency or imbalance, toxicity, or unfavorable environmental factors; illness; sickness; ailment. (TheFreeDictionary.com)

> In humans, "disease" is often used more broadly to refer to any condition that causes *pain, dysfunction, distress, social problems,* or *death* to the person afflicted, or similar problems for those in contact with the person. In this broader sense, it sometimes includes *injuries, disabilities, disorders, syndromes, infections,* isolated *symptoms,* deviant *behaviors,* and atypical *variations* of structure and function, while in other contexts and for other purposes these may be considered distinguishable categories. Diseases usually affect people not only physically, but also emotionally, as contracting and living with many diseases can alter one's perspective on life, and their personality. There are four main types of disease: pathogenic disease, deficiency disease, hereditary disease, and physiological disease. Diseases can also be classified as communicable and non-communicable disease. (*Wikipedia*; italics added)

Here is God's definition for disease:

Anything that sets you not at ease is a disease.

If it causes you to be unsettled, disturbed, shaken, troubled, and uneasy or not at peace, that's a disease. If it infects or affects you spiritually, emotionally, mentally, or physically, then you have a disease. If it causes you to be inflamed, agitated, irritated, aggravated for long periods of time, then you are diseased. A disease can be of the mind, the psyche, and your personality and outlook will be affected and tainted. As I stated in a previous chapter, a clouded mind can see nothing. Simply noted, disease comes to change the original order or design of that which it affects. It degrades, defiles, demolishes, or destroys the wholesomeness of what it takes hold of, leaving only desolation and destruction behind.

Abuse is defined as to forcefully inflict (injure), to be taken without consent (debased), used improperly (misused), to hurt, harm, unjustly accuse (wrong), or pervert that which is wholesome and clean; it means to victimize or pollute another.

Physical abuse could range from assault/battery to aggravated assault (pummeling with fists or an object) to molestation/rape, sexual exploitation (prostitution, human trafficking), or promiscuity, yet in time the body will heal from

> *Effects of Rape Victims of sexual assault are: 3* **times** *more likely to suffer depression* **6 times** *more likely to suffer post-traumatic stress disorder* **13 times** *more likely to abuse alcohol* **26 times** *more likely to abuse drugs* **4 times** *more likely to contemplate suicide - 2.4*

this kind of hurt. Verbal and emotional or spiritual maltreatment is harder to heal because it takes place within a person; it involves the soul and spirit. We can work on the physical by giving it rest, meds, and a change of environment to help it heal, but reaching the wounded soul is a bit tougher. A psychiatrist can treat some things in the psyche (mind), yet if we are going to heal the spirit and soul, we must turn to God. For there is only One (Jesus) who can reach our deepest hurts, sorrows, and grievances. Only He can get to the root of our hurt and pluck it up and pluck it out! Christ alone can eliminate (rid) us of sin's crushing vices (fear, doubt, panic, unbelief, depression, oppression, hatred, bitterness, resentment), expunging (obliterating, obscuring, effacing, rubbing out) it from our lives.

> For this cause the Son of God was manifested, that he might destroy the works of the devil. *(1 John 3:8)*

Christ Jesus alone can unshackle, set loose, deliver, set free, and make us completely whole! He came to seek and to save them which were lost. He alone can give peace to calm every tumultuous raging storm in our minds. He alone is known as the Great Physician. He alone can truly heal the hurt!

Abuse can be like the slam-dunk of assault. It can be a one-time occurrence or a continuous barrage of relentless atrocities that seems to never end. It can leave you feeling not only violated but also stripped, angered, vulnerable, frighten, untrusting, crippled, even powerless. You may go from one vicious cycle to the next, slipping, slinking, sinking, it seems. We go from independency to codependency to dependency, from trusting to doubtful or fearful, from loving to resentful, vengeful, and vindictive. Without ointment applied to the wound, it continues to fester, eating away at the very core of our being. It could and most definitely leads to death—death of the spirit, emotions, and will, producing a wounded soul unable or unwilling to entreat love and embrace life again, as well as physical death.

The Holy Spirit gave me this understanding about what happens when we rely on other things (i.e., the creature rather than the Creator) instead of leaning on

> *The Holy* Spirit *gave me this understanding about what happens when we rely on other things (i.e.,* **the creature rather than the Creator**) *instead of* leaning (**trusting**) *in/on the everlasting arms of* the Lord. *This is what happens when* we lose (**forfeit**) *the freedom Christ gives us and become the slave to sin; our lustful desires. It is what takes place when we try to live in both worlds, deceiving ourselves that* we're just fine. *— 2.5*

the everlasting arms of the Lord. This is what happens when we lose (forfeit) the freedom Christ gives us and become the slave to sin, our lustful desires. It is what takes place when we try to live in both worlds, deceiving ourselves that we are just fine. The following definitions of codependency and dependency came from the Holy Spirit when dealing with our leaning on the arm of flesh versus leaning and depending upon God. This is how the Lord gave it to me:

> Codependency—When we are influenced, enabled, drawn away, and enticed by people, places, or things (our lust, drugs, sex, other people, and the like) that we begin to solely rely on temporary fixes or crutches, relinquishing all responsibility for our own actions or negating that there's anything wrong. It is where we attempt to straddle the fence, so to speak, where we begin to divest ourselves of light, clinging to our own lies, devoid of truth and unable to differentiate the falsehoods from the truth! It is where we coerce others to aid and abet us in our compulsive behavior.

> Dependency—When we are entangled, ensnared, trapped, caught up. Seemingly we have swallowed the hook, line, and sinker! When our lives are fully taken over by the very thing (e.g., alcohol, drugs, illicit sex, other people) we made or used for a temporary fix or crutch; now they become our daily reality or existence.

The Holy Spirit said that this is the result that takes place in our lives when we give in to our own lustful desires, wants, and thoughts. It is from this stance that we attempt to live a life without God, depending on the fruitlessness of our own distorted reasoning to resolve our problems, only to find ourselves more entangled than we were at the beginning. We become like the man whose latter state was worse than when he first received the truth. Jesus warned us about this. In the passage found in Matthew 12:43-45(AMP), the Lord paints a very vivid picture of what happens to us when we choose to be left to our own wit. He drives home this truth, making it perfectly clear why we should allow Him to fill us and why we should not forsake Him in our lives.

> But when the unclean spirit has gone out of a man, it roams through dry [arid] places in search of rest, but does not find any. Then it says, I will go back to my house from which I came out. And when it arrives, it finds the place unoccupied, swept, put in order, and decorated. Then it goes and brings with it seven other spirits more wicked than itself, and they go in and make their home there. And the last condition of that man becomes worse than the first. So also shall it be with this wicked generation.

Does this describe where you are? Is this part of your struggle? If we try to depend or rely on the arm of flesh quicker than trusting in the Lord God our Father, we cause ourselves grave error. This leads us down the wrong path because it is not the order or design for our lives, and in it we miss the mark of God!

There have been countless times in my life where I came to know hurt, a pain sometimes so excruciating, so unbearable that all I knew to do was ask God to swallow me up because I did not desire to live with that kind of pain. I found myself at a point where I wished I could die so as not to feel that pain anymore. I even prayed that a rock would fall on me to hide me. How many of you are in or have ever come to that place? It is where your heart seems to be literally wrenched from your chest or ripped to shreds.

I have known the pain from rape of the mind and of the body, the anguish of the spirit to the point you seem poured out, poured out to the point of empty. Being well acquainted with the pain of being stripped of dignity and self-worth, I began thinking I must be doing something terribly wrong. I thought that surely I would not be going through such agony and wondered why would happen to me. My thoughts were premature and poorly rooted. I believed that nothing that horrible or terrifying would or should ever happen to me because

> [13]for, "Everyone who calls on the name of the Lord will be **saved.**" Romans 10:13 KWSB 2.6

I went to church and I loved God. (Oh, how naive I was! I'll elaborate later!) I did not, like many of us, count in the equation of living—the trials and tests, the proving ground of our lives. I almost brought into the hype or lie that it was my fault, but God showed me that the enemy was trying to destroy me by any means necessary. Satan literally wanted to wipe me out of existence and out of God's story, regardless of whose hands he used!

Every time I would call on God, his love came in and resurrected me, bringing me new life and hope. He restored me not because I was a PK (preacher's kid), not because I said I was a Christian or went to church, not even because I was a minister. God came in just because of his love, plan, thoughts, and perfect will for me to be whole in Him, having health, wealth, and strength. He sent His word and healed my hurt.

> I know the plans and thoughts that I have for you, declares the Lord, plans to prosper you and not harm you, plans to give you hope and a future. Jere. 29:11 — 2.7

In most of those experiences (perhaps you can relate), if I had never known the love of the Father, Son, and Holy Spirit, then I probably would have been like many out there today: full of hate, full of fear, unable to love, unwilling to try, and definitely unforgiving. Perhaps I would have been lost or cut off from existence even. Thank God for his mercy that we are not consumed! *(See Lam. 3:22.)* When one is emotionally or spiritually scarred, it seems to take longer to uproot or erase it. For some it takes years for them to receive their healing from a past hurt. What slows the process of ever being completely healed is our unwillingness to let it go. We continuously drag the chains of hurt, shame, and pain with us from year to year, and it should not be!

Why is that when faced with adversity or opposition, when our problems get too weighty for us, or when we do not understand and cannot reason our way out of the circumstances, situations, or events happening to us, we run from God instead of running to Him?

It is because we forget that He is God the Father, full of mercy, compassion, and love. We forget He desires to be in close relationship with us. The Father pities (watches over, covers) his children as a hen broods over her chicks. Just like Adam and Eve hid from God in the Garden of Eden after they had sinned, so we too try to hide from him. Just as He did in the beginning, God still desires close relationship and fellowship with us today.

Know this: sin will always separate us from God! If we have issues that have not been healed or delivered, then we need to be aware that issues will always do what issues do— they issue!

Isms and Schisms

We also hurt because of erroneous doctrine (teaching) we've received through the years and the bad advice we've accepted as truth. The mere fact is, we've become a people so alienated that it appears we're unreachable, untouchable, unlovable. Perhaps it is from this viewpoint of alienation that we've developed such a gross disdain for the Almighty God (the Heavenly Father and Eternal Creator) that we try out other things to fill up our lives with purpose, possibly trying or hoping to find peace or some sort of happiness in the process. That is why some seek out a new interest (i.e., coexist), a new love (even if it's with the same sex, which is an abomination to God) or something to pacify without closing the door(s) to the past, bringing along with us all the baggage of our woes. Thus, we become contaminated, displaying unhealthy compulsive and undesirable behavior that causes us to act out contrary to the will of God for our lives. Yet still there are those who simply give up because they do not want to hurt anymore, who give up because they do not see or think there's a solution to the problem. It seems there is no way out! We sink to an all-time low. We will give up not even realizing that our healing is as close as the breath we breathe in the arms of a loving and caring Savior, Jesus Christ. Some will even attempt to just go along with everybody so as not to ruffle any feathers, so to speak. Perhaps we try our best to exist with everyone and everything regardless to what it may be, what it represents, or what it is, and yet, God forbid, we still call ourselves Christians. Thus, we come to grips with the term *coexist*.

Coexisting is a movement many who've been hurt, disillusioned, or disenchanted with the church or Christianity follow. It is based on universalism and has a can-we-all-just-get-along core. It is the gospel of acceptance, regardless of what it is, that many have fallen away to. It takes away from the authenticity of God, Jesus Christ, and Holy Ghost (the Holy Triune Godhead: Father, Son, and Spirit). It lumps Christianity and all other beliefs together. Islamism is not Christianity. Wicca/Paganism or the Bab/Bah'ai Faith is not Christianity. Taoism/Confucianism is not Christianity, nor is Judaism. Nor is the peace movement or

> Coexist: a movement which many follow has a can-we-all-just- get-along attitude. It is based on universalism. It takes away from the authenticism of God, Jesus Christ. It lumps Christianity and all other beliefs together.

being supportive of homosexuality/lesbianism (i.e., gay rights) the same as Christianity. You see, all or most of these beliefs have or have had a leader who has lived and died. Only in Christianity do we have One who not only lived and died but arose from the dead with all power in His hand and then ascended into heaven where He sits at the right hand of the Father. That's Jesus! It is only when we believe in Him and His name that we are saved.

Thank the Lord God for salvation through the gift of His Son, Christ Jesus! Thank you, Adonai, for your grace and mercy!

Christianity is ascribed to the lifestyle, attributes, mannerism, and character of those who are and who become the disciples and followers of Jesus Christ. Although Y'shua and the apostles were Jewish, his followers were called Christians not to praise but rather to scorn, ridicule, mock, and put down. It was tagged to them because they truly imitated and replicated the Lord in all their ways. This way (which is Christ Jesus) is who and what his church, bride, and body lives in and is a part of. In Matthew 10:22 (NKJV) Jesus said, "And you will be hated by all for My name's sake. But he who endures to the end will be saved."

On the morning of January 21, 2012, the Holy Spirit began dealing with me concerning these lasts days, our land, and our time and gave me this word to share with his people:

> Are you so blind that you accept whatever you hear, see, or understand so easily to be Christianity, even if it does not look, sound, or appear to be of God?
>
> Are you so easily swayed or duped by those who come loosely wearing the guise of religion that you fall or are taken in by what they are presenting as truth?
>
> Are you fooled or beguiled by the jargon of the day of those who are seeking power and recognition as your redeeming leaders that you cannot see the immorality, injustice, deceit, schisms, and schemes that have been laid to ensnare you?
>
> Why do you accept pompous liars, traitors, and prideful men who do not know the truth neither know of it to reign over you? Will you not seek My face in these matters? Do you yourselves believe them rather than My word? Did you forget that righteousness exalts (upholds) a nation and sin brings reproach to any people? How can one say that they love Me, whom they have not seen, yet hate (choose to ignore or despise) his brother (fellow man) that they see on a day-to-day basis? I tell you that you do not the truth!
>
> Look hard, My sons and daughters, at the disastrous thinking, doctrine, or philosophy that you are accepting from those individuals. Did not My apostle instruct you to think on things that were pure, just, honest, lovely, true, of a good report, and virtuous and to see if it had any praise? Shun, turn away from

such who are themselves polluted and know Me not. These are corrupt individuals who contaminate the truth with lies and deception. They profane My name blasphemously and believe they are right in all their ways; From such depart says the Lord.

Tell them that to be a Christian one must be Christ-like.

True Christians have received the gift of God: eternal life through Jesus Christ.

True people of God are born of the Spirit and of the water. You must be born again!

True Christians are blood-washed and sealed by the Holy Ghost of God.

True Christians walk in the love of God. They do not behave badly.

True Christians love God, as well as themselves and their neighbors, with their all.

True Christians will obey the leading of My Spirit, voice, and my word.

True Christians live by faith (trust, hope) and not by sight (what they see) or by what they can do alone.

True Christians not only have faith in God but faith in Jesus, his only begotten Son.

True Christians will not lie to others; they will do the truth.

True Christians keep the word of God and observe to do it.

True Christians serve the Almighty, Everlasting God wholeheartedly; they do not give lip service.

True Christians are followers of Christ and fishers of men (soul winners of God's kingdom).

True Christians have a relationship with God the Father, Son, and Spirit, not religion.

True Christians are not puffed up and do not attract attention to themselves.

True Christians are humble and yield to the Spirit of God.

True Christians seek God's face, guidance, love, joy, and peace.

True Christians strive to live holy; they do not live as if God does not even exists.

True Christians renders to Caesar what is Caesar's and gives God what belongs to God.

True Christians uphold the law of the land.

True Christians display the grace of God in their words, actions, and deeds.

True Christians are transformed by renewing their minds with the Word of God.

True Christians uphold justice, fairness, equality, and wholesomeness.

True Christians are not seekers of vain glory trying to pocket all they can for themselves or for those who are like them but are eager and willing to be helpers to others.

True Christians will not shut up their mercy but move with compassion, just as the Lord Jesus did.

True Christians seek to be true worshipers of God, worshiping Him in spirit and in truth.

True Christians put their trust (confidence) in the Lord and not in flesh (humankind).

True Christians are not selfish; they do not seek to have it their way.

True Christians never cease to pray, praying always for all things, from the first watch to the fourth watch, making supplication for all saints everywhere.

True Christians are doers of the Word and not hearers only.

True Christians strive to do the right thing (are just, upright before God and man).

True Christians seek to do good rather than evil.

True Christians are faithful to God and with men.

True Christians have forgiving hearts.

True Christians do not hold grudges against others.

True Christians care for those who are weaker than themselves.

True people of God, according to scripture, do not support / do not practice Mormonism, Roman Catholicism, Islamism, Buddhism, homosexuality (gay) or lesbianism, paganism, witchcraft, or the like, but true Christians are children of the Most High God.

True Christians are children of the Light (Jesus) and not children of darkness.

True Christians are not adulterers, idolaters, or rebellious to God.

True Christians are not conformed to this world but are being conformed to the image of Christ Jesus daily.

True Christians are not faultfinders or accusers of the brethren; they do not sow seeds of discord.

This is the word of the Lord for the body of Christ: "He that has an ear to hear let him hear what the Spirit is saying to the church!"

Yes, we do hear a considerable amount of talk about who's a Christian or born-again, but I find that this is more of a label used out of context far too often. There those who are being called evangelical Christians who are causing damage to others who are looking to them for hope as an example in Christ. They are causing this error by not being worthy of the vocation where we are called to holiness and righteousness. They wear the label of Christian as though it should gain them some kind of recognition, a merit badge or a medal of honor to be esteemed within society. They boldly lie before God and man and incite many to wrath, and guile is found in their mouths. It seems they've forgotten it is or was a name of great ridicule given those who patterned their lives after and are followers of the Savior of men: Jesus Christ, the Righteous Lord, Hope of Glory, and King.

Yes, true Christians know that Jesus is the way, truth, and life. True Christians know that only Jesus laid down his life to redeem us and took it back up again when He arose from the grave. True Christians know that He is the Lamb of God who takes away the sins of the world. True Christians have believed that the Lord Jesus is he who said he is, the word made flesh who dwelt among us. True Christians know that without Him, we cannot go to the Father. Neither can we do anything because he is the Life. True Christians know and confess that Jesus is Lord! True Christians know that He is the coming King of Glory, coming to receive his own the bride (His church), and True Christians know that we have victory through Jesus and the forgiveness of sin!

So then without Jesus the Christ being the head, foundation, and chief cornerstone of what you say you believe, then you just might not be a true Christian.

Are you a true Christian? Have you made Jesus, King of kings and Lord of lords, first in your life?

Sometimes we go through hardships because of our disobedience, but there are times that God allows you to go through them for His glory and His perfect will. (Take for instance the incident at the potter's house in Jeremiah 18:4; he marred it in his hands, and he made it again a new vessel.) Here we see the use of the word *marred*, which means to detract from wholeness or perfection or to spoil. The potter's touch describes how God always keeps his hands on us (the vessel). It is we ourselves who forsake the constant keeping and protection of God.

> And I give unto them eternal life; and they shall never perish, neither shall any man pluck them out of my hand. *(John 10:28, KJV)*

> Know ye that the Lord he is God: it is he that hath made us, and not we ourselves; we are his people and the sheep of his pasture. *(Ps. 100:3, KJV)*

I don't profess to know the mind of the Father except that which He through His Spirit reveals to me. I know that we are shaped through the trials, tests, and tribulations we endure in this life. God is the only one who can make us over again. I'm so glad His ways are not our ways and His thoughts are not our thoughts. Isn't it reassuring to know that the Father keeps us in the safety of his hands! Therefore, I am fully persuaded that Jesus Christ is the same yesterday, today, and forever, as the scripture said, and I know He heals the hurt!

Forgive and Forget

We hurt sometimes because we refuse to forgive. We refuse to do so because of our fears, a marginal error! Or if we say we forgive, we keep towing that hurt around with us because in our upbringing, we weren't taught how to forget. I rejoice today in that God cares enough about us that it has been put on record about what forgetting the past will do for us.

> Brethren, I count not myself to have apprehended: but this one thing I do, *forgetting those things which are behind*, and reaching forth unto those things which are before, I press toward the mark for the prize of the high calling of God in Christ Jesus. *(Phil. 3:13-14, KWSB; italics added)*

I've learned that God heals the hurt when we, through Him, are able to forgive and to forget. Our teacher, the Holy Ghost (the Spirit of Truth), will teach us how to forgive, reinstate trust in others, and uproot the weeds of malice and wrath that causes us to compete with one another. God has shown us the greatest example of forgiveness (through His Son, Jesus Christ) that will help us move forward and forget the hurt. In most cases, we have to be shown forgiveness before we are willing to give it, and even after coming into this truth, some still will not forgive. Yet we are instructed by the Lord Jesus to readily bestow it no matter the case. Now if we hold onto those past hurts, woes, sorrows, and the like, we prevent ourselves from moving on, period. If we are unable to let it go, unable to move beyond the hurt, then we cause a major pileup on life's highway not only for ourselves but for everything that's waiting for us to get in our right position and place.

Our best teacher and example is the Heavenly Father, who cast off all our trespasses (transgressions and iniquities, wrongdoing, sin) against Him far from him and remembers them no more! He not only removes them from us, he also forgets them—meaning, He does not hold them as a charge of offense against us. For it is not the Father's will that any perish (cut off, left to die, destroyed), but if we have an unforgiving heart and fail to trust Him and believe his word, we will perish. His greatest desire is that all come unto repentance.

> The Lord is not slack concerning his promise, as some men count slackness; but is longsuffering to us-ward, not willing that any should perish, but that all should come to repentance. *(2 Pet. 3:9, KJV)*

Seeing that God forgave and forgives us, then we ought to also forgive. The Lord Jesus demonstrated this during his ministry and mission. It is also recorded in the Gospels of Matthew and Luke along with Apostle Paul, showing the importance and urgency of our role in activating, implementing, and walking in forgiveness. It is His perfect will that we forgive all who offend us, even our enemies, if we want to be forgiven *(Matt. 6:12-14; Luke 6:34, 7:36-43, 17:3-4, 23:34; Eph. 4:31-32; and Col. 3:13).*

If we reject or neglect that which Christ has given us and choose not to forgive others, then we cannot and will not be forgiven. Because God is not slack and keeps what he's promised, this means he stands by his word. Because of His tremendous love, we therefore have great provision, guarantee, and assurance made for us through the life, death, burial, and resurrection of His Son, Jesus Christ, the Anointed One. The Father doesn't want any of us to be lost. Glory to God! The Lord declares through the prophet Isaiah what happens to us when we disregard his work and the operation of His hands. The Amplified Bible says "in mercy and in judgment." Isaiah states we become captive and are totally oblivious of what takes place when we choose to have no knowledge of God. Because of that, hell has enlarged. What a plan for disaster!

> Therefore my people are gone into captivity, because they have no knowledge: and their honorable men are famished, and their multitude dried up with thirst. Therefore hell hath enlarged herself; and opened her mouth without measure: and their glory, and their multitude, and their pomp, and he that rejoiceth, shall descend into it. *(Isa. 5:13-14, KJV)*

Jesus warns that hell was not made for man when he was teaching about judgment in Matthew 25:31-46. He showed the contrast of those that are on His right hand and those who shall be on his left (verses 31 and 41, KJV). One shall reap the blessing of eternal life while the other reap the curse of everlasting punishment.

> Then shall the King say unto them on his right hand, Come ye blessed of my Father, inherit the kingdom prepared for you from the foundation of the world...

> Then shall he say also unto them on the left hand, Depart from me, ye cursed, into everlasting fire, prepared for the devil and his angels.

It is important to have a forgiving, repentant heart if we want to have a part in God's kingdom. Without this mindset, we can look forward to having a part in hell, eternal punishment, and sorrows beyond our understanding.

Take a look at my case, for example. In 1982, I experienced a living nightmare. By this time so many horrible things had transpired previous to this that I was on the verge of, if not already having, a meltdown (a nervous breakdown because I internalized everything.) It came shortly after my eldest son's father broke trust and stole (the allotment check) from our child. Being angered and enraged, I almost killed him but God! That was the straw that broke the camel's back. This started me on a downward spiral. I became very jittery, emotionally all over the place (scrapped, sifted like shredded wheat), vulnerable, susceptible to anything and everything, it seemed. I was unable to logically cope, focus, or deal with things, functioning only at half capacity. The evening I actually met my youngest son's father was frightening! It was like a dense darkness seemed to surround him. It was like fiery evil eyes burned into the back of my head as he looked at me; fear literally gripped my soul. I caved in to him because I didn't have the fortitude and wasn't stable enough to fight off or reject this undesired, unwanted relationship I wasn't really looking for or ready for, a relationship I didn't need.

He preyed on my emotions, instability, sympathy, and my heart even. He led me to believe he was terminally ill, with only a few months to live. He was subtle, cunning (like our adversary, the devil) and played the part of a godly man before my family, church family, and friends. Sounds like Satan himself, doesn't it? There was a point when it seemed (when things appeared one way, but really were not) my family misunderstood me, but it appeared like he did. I left one evening to go spend the night at a friend's house but went to his instead. He *appeared* to be such a gentleman. He gave us his bed and slept on the couch. Caught in a false sense of security, I lay with him and became impregnated by him. I was so excited because I finally was going have the little girl I'd always wanted! I shared the news with him, and he seemed to be enthused about it too. Soon after he believed he won me over, all hell seemingly broke loose! He became very controlling, extremely demanding, unimaginably obsessive, unrealistically possessive, and overbearingly self-absorbed. It was as if he was trying to dominate my entire life. (It was as if he believed that the world revolved around him.) He had a choke hold of fear on me. I should have gotten a clue then to back away from him. However, I did safeguard my child. I stopped bringing my oldest son around him because he was behaving this way. Although I didn't and was not going to let anything happen to my child, I neglected to do the same for myself.

One day shortly after I shared with him I was pregnant, he almost paralyzed me for life. He turned into a vile, brute beast. In his fit he forced, pushed, and shoved me down onto a couch that didn't give, which caused my spine to jolt upward, pinching a nerve in my upper vertebra. A fiery pain like nothing I had ever felt before hit my lower back. Hot tears ran down my face. With my hand on my back, I tried to leave, but he swiftly stopped me from doing that. Like a predator that has caught its prey, he struck with deadly accuracy and began his attack. He threw me across the room. I hit the side of the bed and almost blacked out as I fell on the floor. Before I could get off the floor, he picked me up and threw me in the middle of the bed. I scooted across the bed till my head was almost touching the floor. Disregarding my pleas for mercy, he forcefully and brutally raped me. It was like I didn't matter; only what he wanted was important to him. Because I didn't give him the response he'd hoped for, he treated and dismissed me like a piece of garbage. He barked at me to leave. I couldn't feel from my waist down after the ordeal. Lying there unable to move, I cried out to God, and he heard me even in that state. It took approximately 30 - 45 minutes (which seemed an eternity) before mobility was restored to the lower half of my body.

That night I lost (miscarried) that child (it was a girl). I was too messed up (embarrassed and ashamed) to tell my own mother or father because I didn't want to disappoint them any further. The following week we went to my brother's graduation from boot camp. Upon returning home, his antics began again. He convinced me he was truly sorry, that he loved and needed me. I fell into the snare set for me. He abducted me, holding me his prisoner for the span of two weeks. He gave or slipped me a mickey or some form of intoxicant in some orange juice. It put me out for two or three days. When I awoke I found that I was bound to the bedposts, stripped of my clothing, and subject to his every whim. Daily he threatened to take my life, stating that if he couldn't have me, then no one could. He threatened to put his "brand" on me like I was his property. And if that wasn't horrendous enough, then ram foreign objects inside me with the intent to ruin me when his usefulness for me was done.

During that time I came literally face-to-face with the spirit of fear. It sucked the very life out of me. It was that same dense darkness I had seen when I first laid eyes on him, the same spirit that had entangled, ensnared, trapped, and held me captive in this horrible setting. It seemed it wanted to swallow me up. Fear had an awful grip on me. It was void of light, warmth, or wholesomeness. It was as the scripture said—full of torment.

> There is no fear in love (dread does not exist); but full grown (complete, perfect) love turns fear out of doors and expels every trace of terror! For fear brings with it the thought of

punishment and [so] he who is afraid has not reached the full maturity of love [is not yet grown into love's complete perfection]. *(1 John 4:18, AMP)*

When it seemed I was un-rescuable at that point, God's perfect love rescued me. The Lord came to my defense. I am so very thankful that God has a way to expel, banish, wipe out, and rid fear from our lives! He did it for me, and I know he'll do it for you!

Eventually, I grew tired of the constant threats and knew only to cry out to God to deliver me. Although I attempted to get away from him, he found me again. That particular night, the Holy Spirit instructed me to tell him these words: "Go ahead and take my life if that's what you really want to do 'cause quite frankly, I'm tired of hearing you tell me day in and day out you're going to kill me." I said it and didn't question it. I closed my eyes and braced myself for the worst, reciting the Lord's Prayer. I didn't know what was going to happen after that, but God did. (I learned that when the Lord is our God, our King, and we surrender and submit to Him, then we can understand the scripture that says, "Stand still and see the salvation of the Lord" *(Exod. 14:13, KJV)*. When the enemy confronts you to destroy you, don't fear or turn to run. Stand on God's word and know the battle is the Lord's. The Lord God will fight for you! See 2 Chronicles 20:15.) He began to literally shake and tremble like a leaf. He lost all his strength and asked repeatedly what I did to him. I knew then that God had rescued me. God delivered me that night out of the hand of the foul man. He does make a way of escape so we can handle it. Glory be to God!

> No temptation has seized you except what is common to man. And God is faithful, he will not let you be tempted beyond what you can bear. But when you are tempted, He will also provide a way out so that you can *stand up under* it. *(1 Cor. 10:13, KWSB; italics added)*

The devil really wanted to take me out (and he has been trying to do so from when I was in the womb), but God has told him no! A few weeks passed. He began stalking me. The enemy had him trying to make a last-ditch effort to possibly take me out. He set up an ambush for me one afternoon and caught me in the jaw with a maximum security padlock.

Thanks be to God my jaw didn't break! I also found out I was pregnant again, this time with my youngest son. Despite all that he put me through, I tried not to hold on to those hurtful things and move forward. Years passed, and although I said I had forgiven him, I found I truly hadn't. Every time I talked with him, I would get enraged and resentful. I strived hard not to transfer my feelings, my hurt or pain, unto my children. I was teaching them to love and forgive their fathers despite what I might've thought or felt toward and about them, yet I wasn't practicing what I preached. I hadn't totally let it go.

One day the word of Lord to me was, "Ask for forgiveness. Ask for it although you were the one wronged, violated, harmed. Don't wait for him to apologize or ask you. When you do this, you'll release My unlimited forgiveness. You'll feel the world seem to roll off you when you ask for forgiveness." I really wanted to object to this one. When the Holy Spirit first spoke this to me, I didn't feel he was worth forgiving. For a moment I couldn't see why I had to be the one to ask for forgiveness. This man seemed to agitate and irritate me every chance he got. He lied concerning our son. He only tried to use him to get me back in his presence. He even had the utmost disrespect for my marriage. Can you imagine being (walking, living, moving as) a ministry vessel and child of God but at the same time promoting and harboring a heart of unforgiveness? God forbid. Being full of unforgiveness and animosity [it built up over a few years] toward him was getting me nowhere. Then finally it hit me. Do it God's way!

I stopped fighting. I ceased fire. Wanting above all things to please God, I did what the Lord had instructed me to do. You know what? It really worked! And today I'm blessed because of it! No longer fear's victim, I am its victor! Because of the Lord Jesus, I've truly overcome!

We cannot hope to move forward in our future if we're always looking back to our past like Lot's wife. Like her (she turned into a pillar of salt), our hearts will become hardened, frigid, ruthless, and unreachable. Forgive the hurt, forget the pain, and remember the lesson that each trial brings us and each test teaches us. Let go! Let God! When we are able to forgive and to release, we able then to be free and clear in our heart, mind, soul, and spirit. And when we are free and clear, then we can look at the lesson (our trials, tests) and help someone else get free.

It is said that you can give without loving (which to me is being heartless, uncaring and detached), yet you cannot love without giving. We should imitate the love of God when giving or dealing with others. Jesus bestowed the Father's enormous heart for us when he said, "For God so loved the world [that's you and I] that He gave His only begotten Son that whosoever believes on Him should not perish [be lost, destroyed, or ruined], but have everlasting life" *(John 3:16, KJV)*.

How great was God's love that he was willing to forgive us.

The scriptures even say that He will remember them no more, our sins and iniquities [our wrongdoing, evil, perverse ways]. "Now when there is absolute remission (forgiveness and cancellation of the penalty) of these [sins and lawbreaking], there is no longer any offering made to atone for sin" *(Heb. 10:17-18, AMP)*.

In Psalm 103:11-13 we find these words: "For as the heaven is high above the earth, so great is his mercy toward them that fear him. As far as the east is from the west, so far hath he removed our transgressions from us. Like as a father pitieth his children, so the Lord pitieth them that fear him."

For us, His love wipes the slate clean, so if God can forgive and forget and love us, then why can't we do the same and permit Him to heal the hurt? That is why this is absolutely true if you will allow God to do it for you: he heals the hurt!

Take this moment and reflect on these words written on April 12, 1994:

Hurt and abused, a victim suffering from years of pain
Feeling victimized by the system, your life full of shame
Shackled by fear, gripped by the horror
You've concluded that nobody cares
All bound up with chains that make heavy
the burden you've tried to bear
Your mind racing with questions,
searching for an answer to find
Is there no deliverance, no solace anywhere?
Undone and without hope, not a song nor a prayer
Oppressed and depressed, your heart full of tears
Lapped by the waves in the Sea of Despair
Can't seem to find any shelter; where will you find rest?
Seems the very walls of life are collapsing all about you
Your faith has been shattered, your love
all shredded and splintered asunder
So torn are the fragments of your life
You believe that now you no longer can trust
Your very prayers seem to be hindered
You've asked is there no way out, nothing that I can do?
Self-esteem and your self-worth is oh so very low
Seems you've lost the right to put up a good fight
So restless, you're tired of tossing every night
The bills mount up, and now your monies run out
Seems your left wondering, When will my change come?
When it seems no one understands or
feels what you're going through
Can participate in the agony that torments you
There is One who can erase the pain
Uproot the hurt that binds you with chains
He'll drench you in his love
He'll loose you from your past
He'll give you joy that will surpass
He'll heal your deepest wound
He'll fill your darkest void
He'll envelop you within the safety of His name
He can do this and more for you
For He's the One who set all men free
So I bid you today let the Lord Jesus have his way

For you He was tried on every point
That He might feel and know what you would have to go through
That is why we cast all our cares upon
Him for he cares for us
He's the out to your in
You don't have to stay hurt

CHAPTER 4

FORGIVENESS

Forgiveness, What Exactly Is It?

In the previous section I shared my experience with forgiving and forgetting. I have learned that so often many of us would rather bury the hatchet with the handle readily accessible to us so that we can pull it out again and go hacking away at whatever or whomever we see need to be trimmed down, but this is not God's way, and neither should it be the way of those who proclaim to be believers—born-again and Christians. God wants us to imitate him in character. That is why we are grafted into His divine nature, which should show forth when we deal with forgiving others. Forgiveness comes not on hollow words or motionless deeds but through the grace that is afforded us by the love of our Lord, Savior, Righteous Judge, and Coming King: Christ Jesus.

Let's take a deeper look at it, shall we?

In the Dictionary.com *to forgive* is defined as the ability to give up resentment against or the desire to punish. It is to pardon, *Forgiveness* is the act or an instance of forgiving, the willingness to forgive, or remission. *Remission* is a release from a debt, pain, disease, a making less. *Remission* is abeyance. Then I looked up *pardon*. It is to release from further punishment, an official document (e.g., God's Word) that grants a pardon. This is where the word *amnesty* comes in, which means to give a general pardon. By having a general pardon, one could be forgiven for anything, any crime, any sin (wrongdoing), no matter how small or how great it may be, except if we take our own life (commit suicide) and blaspheme the Holy Ghost (God's Spirit).

> Therefore I tell you, every sin and blasphemy (every evil, abusive, injurioud speaking, or indignity against sacred things) can be forgiven men, but blasphemy against the [Holy] Spirit shall not and cannot be forgiven. And whoever speaks a word against the Son of Man will be forgiven, but whoever speaks against the

Spirit, the Holy One, will not be forgiven, either in this world
and age or in the world and age to come. *(Matt. 12:31-32, AMP)*

This is the only thing that God will not forgive us for: trespassing against his Holy Spirit, who is also the Spirit of Life. Because the Lord, the Author of Life, made us in his own image and after his likeness, we should not take life for granted. God breathed His Spirit into man's nostrils, and man became a living soul *(Gen. 1:26, 2:7)*. The psalmist concurs with this, saying, "Know ye that the Lord he is God: it is he that hath made us, and not we ourselves; we are his people, and the sheep of his pasture" *(Ps. 100:3, KJV)*. Seeing that we are not the Author of Life but his children, then we do not have

> 'And the Lord God formed man out of the dust of the ground, and breathed into his nostrils the breath of life: and man became a living soul. Gen. 2:7 -3.2

the right or authority to take (end, cut short) our lives. God holds us accountable for the life he has given us to live. Extinguishing one's life is not something any one of us can tell God the Father we are sorry for doing. For this sin, we will not and cannot be pardoned. In doing this, we say to Him that we reject the gift of life he has given us.

The apostle John warned us against this and said it was not something we could go to God about on anyone's behalf. Here is what the scripture says:

> If anyone sees his brother [believer] commit a sin that does not [lead to] death (the extinguishing of life), he will pray and [God] will give him life [yes, He will grant life to all those whose sin is not one leading to death]. There is a sin [that leads to death: I do not say that we should pray for that All unrighteousness is sin, and there is sin which does not [involve] death [that may be repented of and forgiven.] *(1 John 5:1617, AMP)*

Action or Deed?

Ever wonder or ask why we are not taught how to vent what we feel? Or why we should not hold in our feelings? Holding in eventually leads to an outbreak of anger. Or maybe it is even compulsiveness, which is not forgiveness. Holding in will cause an individual to implode on oneself. We walk around with a facade, saying "I'm fine" or "I'm all right," knowing all to well that we are broken and truly need to be healed. We try to cover it by hiding behind our masks. We begin to seep. We go from seeping, to oozing, to gushing. This happens because of our leaky heart issues, which we refuse to deal with or do not know how to deal with. We may hold it in so long because we don't know how to let go or to get free of our hurt. Eventually, the dam will break, and we will lose it.

This should never be the stance of the believer. We should be ready to forgive those who trespass against us, like the Lord Jesus showed us in the model prayer he taught his disciples.

Jesus said that we are His disciples if we continue in his word *(John 8:31)*. When we are hurt, is our first reaction to withhold forgiveness? Is the course of action we take getting back at the person(s) who wronged us instead of making peace with them? If we are easily and readily provoked, then we are not walking in or practicing forgiveness. Neither do we have the peace that Jesus gave us. Scripture tells us that we should be willing to forgive no matter the offense, issue, or hurt. Jesus admonished us to put it in action daily no matter how many times we are wronged. Be always ready to forgive. The act of forgiveness must become a natural occurrence, just as innate as our five senses, which are needed for the correct functioning of the body.

Perhaps you are puzzled in looking for headers. Are you wondering if God is concerned about your cares? Do you recognize Him as your Heavenly Father? Are you possibly wondering if God is real and if he will take the pain away? Will God hear you? Will He answer when you talk to Him? Maybe these questions are similar to those that have bombarded the mind when you are confronted with the opportunity to forgive or not to forgive:

First, how many people can truly say that they are willing to forgive someone when they are hurt by them?

The willingness to forgive does not depend or rely on how close you are related to a person or how long they have worked with or gotten acquainted with you, even if they have walked and shared much with you throughout life. The person could be a total stranger, but you (the believer) still have to be ready to forgive. We are compelled by the Lord to forgive if we want to be forgiven. And the scripture says, "Forbearing one another, and forgiving one another, if any man has a quarrel against any; even as Christ forgave you; so also do ye" *(Col. 3:13, KJV)*.

Second, how many of us can learn to forgive ourselves after we have received forgiveness? How many of us would truly be honest with ourselves? How many of us would be honest with God the Father above and ask for forgiveness?

We can be our own worst enemy and beat up on ourselves, condemning ourselves even after the Lord has redeemed us, a trick of our adversary, the devil! The scripture says, "If we confess our sins, he is faithful and just to forgive us our sins, and to cleanse us from all unrighteousness" *(1 John 1:9, KJV)*. All we must do is open our mouths and confess (surrender) it to Jesus. He will deliver you!

Oh yes, God is concerned about us. If we sincerely seek Him, we will surely find him. Know this, we must believe that He is God! If we will trust in Him, we will find we can be assured of His word and know that He will answer us with His Spirit. He forgives, and he saves!

Let's take a moment to clear our minds of any debris or stress from the day and take a load off in the process. Follow the steps below:

It goes like this: relax, relate, release.

Relax, let it go or let go. For instance, take three deep cleansing, calming breaths. Breathe in (inhale through your nose). Now hold it in for a moment. Now

> When we are relaxed, free and can connect: not only can we see dearer, but we can comprehend and assess the situation or circumstance better. When WE aren't relaxed, can't identify, connect are bound: then we'll only operate from a clouded perspective. - 3.3

release. Breathe out slowly through your mouth. With the last breath, try holding it in a little longer and letting it out very slowly. Bring up those things that have you agitated, overwhelmed, frustrated, or a bit confused at the present. Clear your heart and mind as you exhale.

Relate means to connect, link, associate, identify. See how the situation or circumstance benefits you. See the bigger picture. Take from each experience the positive *only*. Allow the Holy Spirit to filter out or leave behind the negative aspects. Get into the solution, and don't dwell on the problem.

Release means to be set free, loosed, unhindered, unchained, unhooked, let go. Remember this: he that has the Son (Jesus) is free indeed. If you want to be free and stay free, then you got to forgive!

Are you feeling relaxed now? Were you able to release? (I got this technique for my dear friend, Wanda K.)

Before we react, take the time to get a clear perspective before taking any action and moving out of fierce anger instead of a heart of forgiveness.

When dealing with forgiveness, how we respond is everything. Are we trying to fill the voids in our lives by searching and searching, looking for something to grasp or hold on to? It seems that every time something or someone hurts us (if it is not resolved and healed), we'll go from one thing to another. We look for approval (we seek to be validated), love (to be reciprocated in whomever or whatever), peace (because hurt brings about separation, along with some sort of confusion and despair), joy (happiness), and understanding (clarity) in all the wrong places. We can find love, forgiveness, comfort, hope, peace, joy, refuge, freedom, healing, and so much more in God's word. We can find restoration, reconciliation, and renewal too. It only occurs when we are willing to cross that threshold of pain and its growing depression and when we are willing to go beyond the barriers of hurt, denial, and sin. That is when we can find hope, which makes us not ashamed, and peace that surpasses our understanding. We can find love greater than all our knowledge and joy unspeakable (too wondrous for words) and be full of God's glory (*Rom. 5:1-5; Phil. 4:6-8; Eph. 3:17-19*).

Our past hurts are like gigantic chains that bind and hinder our development. Our growth, it seems, is stumped, stifled, smothered because we, being human, rely on our own strength. It seems we forget or do not realize we have a Heavenly Father who cares for us. Whenever we don't relinquish hurt, grief, or pain into His hands, we operate with stinking thinking. Christ Jesus who knew no sin became sin for us. He was tried (tested) on all points; he is acquainted with our pain and sufferings. When I think about how so many talk show hosts/ hostesses use the pain that people hold in (mostly from their childhood years) as their topics of the day, I feel very saddened—sad that in our country, we thrive on hearing about the hurt, the fears, the grief, and pain of others And mortified because our media magnifies the negative more than the positive. We do so as if there is no other way we can entertain or amuse ourselves.

How truly horrendous it is to live in a land where we are teaching and demonstrating to the world and our children that the only way to solve anything is to go on national television. We go there to either discuss, argue about it, or act out obscenely and profanely with one another. We do so in hopes that through the process and finite counseling of our minds, it will be settled, but in some instances it never gets resolved. Seemingly in overdrive, this way ends

> *Do not be deceived: God cannot be mocked. A man reaps what he sows Galatians 5:7 NIV — 3.4*

in injury, leaving the already fragile wounded heart, mind, and spirit dashed like powder in the wind. I pray that someone with the boldness of the Holy Ghost would stand up and speak in truth for once, that someone who truly knew God as Lord, Father, Healer, Lover, Savior, and Comforter would intercede, not those so-called imitations, false prophets, and God haters who perpetrate, taint, and use God as a token or toy to be played with. Maybe then we would send out the right messages, the right signals to our youth and to the world. This is so needed in a society where it seems apparent there is no give, only take. My desire is that all would come to know that God still forgives, loves, cares, delivers, and that He heals the hurt!

Burying the Hatchet

At what focal point do we zoom in on our pain? Is it solely based upon past fears, hurts, and old wounds that never really healed? None of us enjoy the pangs of pain tugging at our bodies, our hearts, or our souls, yet it is our pain that we do not realize our adversary, the devil, thrives upon. He lives and grows more powerful against us when we give in to our pains, hurts, and fears. He becomes stronger against us when we do not realize whom we serve and whose we are or when we do not realize what arsenal is at our disposal. That's why the Bible says that fear has torment but that perfect love casts out all fear. Jesus is our high priest, and he has felt all that we would ever go through for He was tried on all points. He knows the good, the bad, the sorrows, the grief and pain. As the prophet Isaiah described Him, "He is despised and rejected of men, a man of sorrows, and acquainted with grief: Surely he hath borne our griefs, and carried our sorrows: and with His stripes we are healed" *(Isa. 53:3-5, KJV).* Go over to Matthew, where we can back this up. Chapter 8 verse 17 reads, "That it might be fulfilled which was spoken by Esaias the prophet, saying, Himself took our infirmities, and bare our sickness." If Jesus carried it, why are you carrying it?

Why not turn our hurts, our all (everything) over to Him who died for us, to Jesus, who said in Matthew 11:28-30 KJV, "Come unto me, all ye that labour and are heavy laden and I will give you rest. Take my yoke upon you, and learn of me; for I am meek and lowly in heart: and ye shall find rest unto your souls. For my yoke is easy, and my burden is light."

The apostle Peter saw the importance and urgency in knowing how, when, where, and what we should release. In 1 Peter 5:7 KJV, he wrote, "Casting all your care upon him; for he careth for you." We too should fall to rest in His loving arms, securely hidden in safety of His breast (bosom), where in His love we will find peace, joy, and rest, where forever, if we continue in Him, we are blessed.

Why is it so hard for us to forgive? Is there something or some grounds that we should base our judgment upon, or are we unbiased in our judgment? Matthew 7:1-2 reads, "Judge not, that ye be not judged. For what judgment ye judge, ye shall be judged: and with what measure ye mete, it shall be measured to you again."

The Bible teaches us to be swift to hear, slow to speak, and slow to anger to be ready to give an answer to every man that asks of us. *(Read James 1:19 and 1 Peter 3:15.)* Yet how many of us are actually uncritical of the next, are not superficial with our brother/sister, or are unpretentious with one another? How many of us really possess genuine love for our fellow man, as well as can walk together in love and go down into the depths of love with someone else? Mostly, all our neighbors (those we interact with and come in contact with on a daily basis) desire from us is our ability to show compassion, love, joyfulness, sympathy, empathy, justice, the willingness of a helping hand, a friend whom will understand, and the evidence of fruit (works, spiritual attributes displayed in our character).

Why must our love be so conditional? God the Father loves us unconditionally. For us He gave His only Son, the only begotten Son of the Father, he who freely laid down his life that none should perish (be lost, cast away, cut off without remedy) but gain (have) everlasting life. God is no respecter of persons, so why are we? This was a love so great and so strong that it alone dissolved the chains of sin, death, hell, and the grave. Chains from generations upon generations that held every man and every woman enslaved. So deep and so vast was God's love that he emancipated all. He cared not what the cause of our shortcomings was. For us, He pardoned. Yes, He forgave. I heard that though the justice in Him cried out for a sentence (punishment), the mercy in Him replied with an answer that none should be lost—no, that none would have to die. He loved us regardless. He loves us despite of ourselves. *(See 2 Peter 3:9, John 3:15, and Romans 5:5-10.)*

Christ died so none would have to pay the price for sin, of a truth none of us could have for we were not worthy enough. He who knew no sin took our place. He alone knew our fate. He cast off our transgressions, took away all our iniquities, blotted out all our sins. God removes them from us and remembers them no more. This is what is meant by the verse "He throws them into the Sea of Forgetfulness" *(Jer. 31:34, Micah 7:19 AMP).*

> This is the agreement (testament, covenant) that I will set up and conclude with them after those days, says the Lord: I will imprint My laws upon their hearts, and I will inscribe them on their minds (on their inmost thoughts and understanding), He then goes on to say, And their sins and their lawbreaking I will remember no more. *(Heb. 10:16-17, AMP)*

He wiped our slate clean, giving to us a new day in Him. He, with his love, covered us completely, casting off our garments of reproach. We thus became a new creature in Him.

> Therefore if any person is [ingrafted] in Christ (the Messiah) he is a new creation (a new creature altogether): the old [previous moral and spiritual condition] has passed away. Behold, the fresh and new has come! *(2 Cor. 5:17, AMP)*

Our reward? Life everlasting. Only through Christ we can win.

Walking in Forgiveness, More Than Saying I'm Sorry

I believe that forgiveness is important to God. His desire for us to walk in forgiveness and continue in a right relationship and fellowship not only with Him but also with others is very great. It is a vital, potent, and unequivocal part of every believer's character and heart. I believe that is why Jesus put great emphasis on us having the ability through Him, his word, and his love for us working in us to forgive others. Here is a prophetic message on forgiveness:

> *The word of the Lord today is:*
> Forgive!
>
> *Given on August 22,2008*
> – 3.5

The word of the Lord today is *forgive*!

Often we find ourselves in a position to forgive or not to. We can disobey His word and go on as if we are okay when the truth is we are in total violation of the spiritual law of forgiveness.

Jesus said, "For if ye forgive men their trespasses, your heavenly Father will also forgive you. But if ye forgive not men their trespasses, neither will your Father forgive your trespasses" *(Matt. 6:14-15, KJV)*.

> Judge not, and ye shall not be judged: condemn not, and ye shall not be condemned: forgive and ye shall be forgiven: Give and it shall be given unto you; good measure; pressed down, and shaken together, and running over, shall men give into your bosom. For with the same measure that ye mete withal it shall be measured to you again. *(Luke 6:37- 38, KJV)*

It is like the law of gravity: what goes up must come down. The latter part of verse 38 tells us about how we can expect to receive, whether we've dealt it out sparingly (in a miserly way, frugally) or in abundance (cheerfully). I would like to reiterate this: you do reap what you sow!

> Be not deceived; God is not mocked: for whatsoever a man soweth, that shall he also reap. For he that soweth to his flesh shall of the flesh reap corruption; but he that soweth to the Spirit shall of the Spirit reap life everlasting. And let us not be weary in well doing: for in due season we shall reap, if we faint not. As we

have therefore opportunity, let us do good into all men, especially unto them who are of the household of faith. *(Gal. 6:7-10, KJV)*

You know the saying, "What goes around comes around!" And sometimes it comes back triple, seemingly with a vengeance!

It would be a horrific mistake on our part to have an unforgiving heart, to hate or detest our brother or our sister and still say we love God.

If anyone says, "I love God," yet hates his brother, he is a liar. For anyone who does not love his brother whom he has see, cannot love God, whom he has noe seen. And he has given us this command: Whoever loves God must also love his brother. *(1 John 4:2021, KWSB)*

Forgiveness plays a vital role in our living successfully for and in God. It is a tremendous part of our obedience to God. I simply do not know how one can name the Lord Jesus and refuse to forgive. We do not fully realize the jeopardy we put our souls in. Jesus said in Matthew 10:28 (KJV), "And fear not them that can kill the body, but are not able to kill the soul: but rather fear Him which is able to destroy both body and soul in hell."

Now is not the time to be playing Russian roulette (the game where you cock the pistol and hope that you miss the bullet) with your eternity. It is time to be obedient, to love and trust God the Father with everything and all that is within us. We must affirm His word and conform to his ways; we must be transformed by his word.

I BESEECH you therefore, brethren, by the mercies of God, that ye present your bodies a living sacrifice, holy, acceptable unto God, which is your reasonable service. And be not conformed to this world: but be ye transformed by the renewing of your mind, that ye may prove what is that good, and acceptable, and perfect will of God. *(Rom. 12:1-2, KJV)*

When we submit or surrender our will, our agenda, and our ways to God's will, agenda, and ways, we arm ourselves likewise with the mind of Christ.

Let nothing be done through strife or vainglory: but in lowliness of mind and let each esteem other better than themselves. Look not every man on his own things, but every man also on the things of others.

Let this mind be in you, which was also in Christ Jesus: Who being in the form of God, thought it not robbery to be equal with God: But made himself of no reputation, and took upon him the form of a servant, and was made in the likeness of men: And being found in fashion as a man, he humbled himself and became obedient unto death, even death of the cross. *(Phil. 2:5-8, KJV)*

It matters not what it is or how minute or how great the thing is. We *must* forgive!

Jesus said in Matthew 18:21-22 (KJV; italics added), "Then came Peter to him, and said, Lord how oft shall my brother sin against me, and I forgive him? Till seven times? Jesus said unto him, *'I say not unto thee, Until seven times: but, Until seventy times seven.'*"

The possibility for forgiveness is endless. We have to be willing to forgive or ask for forgiveness, even if we were the one violated. He came to make us the victor and not the victim. You dethrone or usurp power from the thing or person who needs forgiveness when you forgive. Sin, shame, and bondage no longer have power over you because of your obedience to God's word.

When we refuse to obey the voice of the Lord, the scriptures says in 1 Samuel 15:22-23 (KJV), "And Samuel said, Hath the Lord as great delight in burnt offerings and sacrifices, as in obeying the voice of the Lord? Behold, to obey is better than sacrifice, and to hearken than the fat of rams. For rebellion is as the sin of witchcraft, and stubbornness is as iniquity and idolatry."

This should not be! Then next the prophet Samuel said to Saul was, "Because thou hast rejected the word of the Lord, he hath also rejected thee from being king."

Forgiveness brings forth His mercy, but an unforgiving or disobedient heart will propel us into His justice or judgment (Rom. 6:23), which demands death. It hinders our prayers:

> If I regard iniquity in my heart, the Lord will not hear me.
> *(Ps. 66:18, KJV)*

What position will you take? Obedience and forgiveness, where there is life, or disobedience and an unforgiving heart, which ends horribly, as the scriptures says in *Proverbs 16:25 (KJV)*: "There is a way that seemeth right unto a man, but the end thereof are the ways of death." Will you be accepted by God, or will you be rejected?

FORGIVE!

There's a thin line between love & hate
Please make no mistake
If you have Christ living in you
Then forgive me as He forgives you
Forgiveness is a special tool
A priceless gem for us to use
If we learn to live by this rule
Then there wouldn't be any dying in our schools
Love covers a multitude of faults

So please pour in the love of God like salt
If you have an ear, please hear
Not with your head, but with your heart
When God forgave us
He blots out every part
His forgiveness takes away all our wickedness
As far as the East is from the West
And He cast them into the Sea of Forgetfulness
If I regard iniquity in my heart
Then the Lord will not hear me
If I say I love the Lord, whom I have not seen
And hate my brother or my friend that I do see
How can I say I have the love of God in me?
For through the tests, though I've made a mess
I've learned the key
To open the door for me is forgiveness, don't you see
He who love the best, loves the greatest
Forgiveness is an everyday thing
It is what makes my little heart sing
Because He forgives me when I forgive you
So in closing, I say to you
As oft as you can,
As quick as you can,
Whenever you can,
No matter what you can;
Always forgive
Cause it's the only way to live...
F O R G I V E!!!

CHAPTER 5

WHERE THE KILLING STOPS, LOVE BEGINS

Long ago, in a time when you could leave your doors and windows open, we lived more in harmony. In fact, we would sleep all night with them open. Life was simpler, cleaner, wholesome. Children were innocent. People had morals and were decent. It was a time when things were less expensive and you hardly ever heard of crime. Kids *didn't* kill kids! It simply was unheard of. Our neighborhoods were built on friendship. People trusted one another. People shared with one another. Families were closely knitted together. Your neighbors watched your kids for you while you were out. Then our parents. Children respected community took care of its children. The world wasn't so full of chaos.

Children were disciplined, and parents didn't have to worry about being fined or jailed for it. Children were children, and our parents were their elders and those who were in authority over them and desired to pattern their lives after them.

Children were mannered and obedient too. Prayer was not only in our homes but also in the schools. Compared to now, it was a time of peace. Those were the good ol' days, huh? Did we make the right choice in allowing that which our country was based

> Here's what the Word says about sparing the rod: "He that spares his rod [of discipline] hates his son, but he who loves him disciplines diligently and punishes him early" (Prov. 13:24, AMP).

on (principles and statutes) to be removed (e.g., the institution of prayer, loss and decrease of parental rights, discipline with the rod of correction). Did we spoil the child by sitting back and doing nothing? God's word specifically and emphatically gives us instruction about discipline. It shows us why it is important in the shaping and molding of character, personality, good judgment, soundness of heart, and wholesome behavior of our children.

> The rod and reproof give wisdom, but a child left undisciplined brings his mother to shame...Correc.t your son, and he will give you rest; yes he will give delight to your heart. *(Prov. 29:15, 17, AMP)*

Did we lose our voice, perspective, and respect by complaining about things but never becoming part of the solution? Did we wait too late to do something? God forbid.

What of Innocence?

Kids didn't have to worry about ducking for cover and dodging bullets flying at night or on their playgrounds. We didn't have to worry about our children committing suicide. Our families were more structured. Our children weren't taken over by fear, depression, or oppression.

Innocence n 1: freedom from guilt or sin through being unacquainted with evil: BLAMELESSNESS: also freedom from legal guilt 2: freedom from guile or cunning: integrity, decency – 4.2

Even the *youths shall faint* and be weary, and the young men shall utterly fall. *(Isa. 40:30, KJV; italics added)*

But they that wait upon the Lord shall renew their strength: they shall mount up with wings as eagles; they shall run, and not be weary; and they shall walk; and not not faint. *(Isa. 40:31, KJV)*

Dying from taking a drug overdose wasn't their pastime. Taking drugs wasn't an issue of the day. Inhaling paint thinner, glue, aerosols, or hoofing air dusters wasn't the thing to do. They weren't into slashing themselves either. Nor were they into becoming alcoholics. It was unheard of! Children didn't drink anything but water, iced tea, Kool-Aid, or lemonade. Children didn't commit diabolical and heinous crimes. Children weren't so rebellious. We had real babysitters, but then the television became the sitter. Our kids never had so much violence to watch. Our kids never had so much violence, degradation, and deprivation to absorb. Parent spent hours reading to them instead. Children played with their friends, and they would play for hours. Children once loved being outdoors. They didn't get bored easily. They didn't lose interest in what they were doing. They weren't being taken, ensnared, or entangled in their own craftiness, folly, and poor judgment. They weren't easily distracted. Now their place of fascination is being indoors, doing their thing. Have you heard of the saying "An idle mind is the devil's workshop?" Sad to say, it's true.

Children weren't in such a hurry to have serious relationships. They weren't trying to hook up or get with it. They weren't so engulfed with television, video games, cell phones, iPads, iPods, mp3s, being on social networks, belonging to a gang, the Internet, perversion (dabbling and immersing themselves in incest, sodomy, homosexuality, or lesbianism), or pornography.

[A Total of 90% of children 8-16 have viewed pornography online]. - Children Internet Pornography Statistics

1. Average age of 1st Internet exposure: 11 yrs. old
2. Largest consumer: 35-49 age group
3. 15-17 yr. olds having multiple hard-core exposures: 80% 8-16 yr. olds having viewed porn online: 90% (mostly while doing homework)
4. 7-17 yrs. olds who would freely give out home address: 29%

5. 7-17 yr. olds who would freely give out email address: 14%
6. Children character names linked to thousands of porn links: 26 (Including Pokémon and Action Man).

Tweeting or texting wasn't a national pastime. We didn't have so many children suffering from ADHD (attention deficit/hyperactivity disorder). They were more attentive. Children weren't making headlines for doing evil things. Parents looked forward to developing their children to be positive, productive, prosperous, and full of potential. They were more concerned with their growth and mastery academically, creatively, culturally, physically, even spiritually. Parents were invested in their children's activities, not just the stock of their own lives. Children were eager to learn, active, and full of wonderment. Children honored and obeyed their father and mother. Children were children.

These scriptures speaks about honoring father and mother. They speak of what and how children should behave and what happens when we refuse to align ourselves with God's divine order for the family:

> For God commanded; saying, Honor thy father and mother; and, He that curseth father or mother, let him die the death. *(Matt. 15:4, KJV)*

> CHILDREN, OBEY your parents in the Lord: for this is right. Honor thy father and mother; which is the first commandment with promise; That it may be well with thee, and thou mayest live long on the earth. *(Eph. 6:1-3, KJV)*

> Children, obey your parents in all things: for this is wellpleasing unto the Lord. Fathers, provoke not your children to anger, lest they be discouraged. *(Col. 3:20-21, KJV)*

Back in the day, teenage pregnancy was almost unheard of. Children weren't having children. Parents didn't worry about children being sexually active or sexually promiscuous. Children weren't engaged in all manners of perversion either. They weren't trying to get their freak or swerve on (meaning, heavily into sexual intercourse, into oral or anal sex). They weren't occupied with knocking boots, in other words. It wasn't a notion to be considered. We didn't have to deal with them contracting or transmitting STDs and the AIDS virus spreading rapidly among them. There just was no such thing. On a large scale, they weren't considered an object of rape or sexual assault either. Parents didn't have to worry about sexual predators seeking their children out for their

15% of sexual assault and rape victims are under age 12.

The desire of the slothful kills him; for his hands refuse to labor. He covets greedily all day long, but the [uncompromising! y] righteous gives and docs not withhold. Prov. 21:25-26 AMP; see also. 2 Cor. 9:6-IO – 4.6

twisted lustful fulfillment and pleasure. We once lived in a time when our children's innocence was intact, untainted, undisturbed, and undefiled, but now all that has changed.

Nowadays, you can't tell who's who in our society. Little girls want to be grown women, and little boys are told they are men. It's all out of order. Our children go about acting the part of something they're not. Children didn't think themselves to be so wise. They didn't think themselves invincible. They don't give respect but certainly want it. Our children don't have a clue about the law of reciprocity (reaping what you sow). In order to receive, you must be willing to give! They simply don't understand the concept that you must give respect in order to gain it. Instead, rebellion, stubbornness, and foolery indicates their choice of behavior. They've chosen the worst fads to latch on to (e.g., wearing saggy pants, tattooing, using slang/ profanity) to express themselves. They've come to a place where they would rather take or have it handed to them than work for what they want, desire, or require. Proverbs 21:25-26 speak against this way of living. *(See also 2 Cor. 9:6-10.)*

Children Affected by Sexual Assault & Rape

29% are age 13-17.
44% are under age 1R.
80% are under age 3G.

12-34 are the highest risk years.

Where did our moral leaders go? Is it something in the water? Crime involving our children is now on the rise. Our children are being slaughtered. Whether by their own hands, because of abuse, or from another source, our children are vanishing. Why are we so apt to hurt ourselves? Most of us that came up in the sixties grew up with the race riots. Bigotry and prejudice were our hard-core issues, not our children hurting or killing one another. I remember a time when children played hard, fought hard, and loved even harder. The age of innocence seems all but vanished, without

Girls ages 16-19 are 4 times more likely than the general population to be victims of rape, attempted rape, or sexual assault, - 4.5b

any traces of recovery in view. Once where babies came into the world with their eyes closed for several days, now they arrive bright-eyed, trying to talk, and fully aware of their surroundings. They come all ready to take on the world but seemingly without the knowledge that they are still babies. They appear wiser, yet they are weaker in that they don't weather or handle life well.

Where Did We Go Wrong?

Remember back on April 26, 1999, when Lanetta King, a brilliant teenager, was shot and killed by a stray bullet? Think of it, a child with nothing but hopes and dreams of a wonderful future, a child embarking on womanhood, a child who will not be able to contribute her aspirations or her ideas. Never again will the world hear the joyful sounds of her

Children killed by Handguns

*43% of households in USA that have **children** also have handguns in them*
*10 children are shot and killed every **day***
***1** child will die every day from **an** accidental gun **shot** -4.7*

laughter or be able to comfort her when she cries or console her when she's angry.

How many Lanetta Kings must there be in this country before we can get a grip on this senseless killing spree? Why should our children have easy access to guns and semi and fully automatic weapons? What can we do to change this? Where is the legacy that we are leaving behind? Where has our children's laughter gone? It does my heart good to see a group of children having a good romp. To see them play well together outside my door or on a courtyard, especially in a time when our children are killing each other off. We don't have to worry so much about an incurable disease wiping them out; they're doing that by their own hands, and it seems that we do little or nothing but just stand by, watch, and allow it to happen.

We grew up a different set of values. We had family- oriented entertainment versus the self-promoting, self-serving, and self-pleasing media outlets of today. We learned some life lessons from the Cleavers *(Leave It to Beaver)*, *The Andy Griffith Show*, *My Three Sons*, *Father Knows Best. The Brady Bunch*, the Evans *(Good Times)*, Bill Cosby *(The Cosby Show)*, and other shows like them, though comedic at times, have displayed values and demonstrated how we should function, love, cheer, laugh, cry, and live together as a family. But the process of time and our growing dependency on technology (feeding our insatiable hunger for what's in and what's out), we've lost our morals and values and lowered our standards. Through the years we factored out God, his word, and prayer in our daily lives as if we can make it on our own. We've stop praying together. We've stop caring about one another. We've done so against better judgment for what sounds, looks, feels good instead of that which is good, wholesome, and right.

The scripture says, "Train up a child in the way he should go; and when he is old, he will not depart from it" *(Prov. 22:6 KJV)*.

We seem to have forgotten that principle. We desire the quick, instant, ready-made, and right-now thing rather than that which we would have to wait on or work for. We prefer the quick fix, the temporary patchwork rather than the permanent and sure solution. We look for that which appeals to the senses rather than enriching and fortifying our relationship with God. We shun sound doctrine for utter nonsense that have no real basis. We cling to shreds of truth (lies) and thrive off of gossip spreading this poison like wildfire. We indulge in frugal idleness rather than readiness and productivity.

You know, I read this story once about two brothers, two loves, and one great loss. Both had loving parents. Both were industrious. One raised cattle. The other was an agricultural whiz. One day, there was a great big presentation. Both of the brothers brought their best work to be presented. One presentation was accepted, the other rejected. (It didn't meet the requirements or the standards that were set). Because of this, one brother was eaten by anger, jealousy, envy and took his brother's life. He asked the question, "Am I my brother's keeper?" He didn't see his role in being responsible for his actions. We see a lot of that going on today. We, like this brother, have grown insensitive, uncaring about our fellow man.

Jesus said, "And because of iniquity shall abound, the love of many shall wax cold" *(Matt. 24:12, KJV)*.

Out of this insensitivity, we have thus produced children who are immature (not completely developed, unskilled, unlearned), irreverent (no regard for God or man), and irresponsible (having no accountability.) Because of this insensitivity, we've produce bullies. A bully (a gangster, goon, thug) is a person who is habitually cruel to those who are weaker. Ecclesiastes 12:1 will definitely help us keep our eyes focused on God. Recently while watching a children's program *(Green Screen Adventures)*, they read a poem titled "Stop the Violence" written by Dakota of Whistler Elementary. It was most profound and spoke directly to the sentiments (heart) of this chapter. While searching the Internet, I found another poem having the same title by a youth named Engrid Malone. It too spoke out just as loudly and profoundly as Dakota's did:

> *REMEMBER NOW thy Creator in the days of thy youth, while the evil days come not, nor the years draw nigh, when thou shalt say, I have no pleasure in them. – 4.8*

Stop the Violence

Two youths on a corner
smoking marijuana,
got into a fight
someone died that night.
Stop the violence!!
Young children with guns and knives
selling drugs to make it in life,
failing to realize that their actions
will not bring them satisfaction.
Stop the violence!!
Stealing cars and robbing stores
making easy money is the life they prefer,
never having to work
ending up six feet under dirt.
Stop the violence!!
Fathers molesting daughters
robbing them of their innocence,
now things will never be the same
have to hang their heads in shame.
Stop the violence!!
We need to work together,
to heal our community
we cannot do it alone, together we can...
Stop the violence!

(Engrid Malone)

My prayer for ourselves and our children is that we would take heed wherever we are, whatever we find ourselves doing at all times.

Don't forget God! Don't leave God out of the equation. Don't try to live this life without Him. Let us keep God first in our lives!

Building Character

Where did all the strong role models disappear to? Those who portrayed positive roles for children end up becoming their predators instead. What a shame to even be mentioned. There used to be a time when our children looked up to the police and wanted to be policemen when they grew up. They were the ones who shielded and protected the people. We played cops and robbers when we were little, but not anymore. We've become fearful of them instead. Most of us have lost our

> **Character n 3:** a distinguishing feature: ATTRIBUTE 4: the complex of mental & ethical traits marking a person or group 7: one reputation: good name 8: moral excellence: decency, goodness, honesty, integrity, morality, righteousness – 4.9

confidence in the judicial system because it doesn't seem to work for the injured party. It seems to exonerate the crime and the criminal and exploit the poor victim. The way the O. J. Simpson trial was handled was a complete sham. It seemed that the media had blown it out of proportion. Most folks don't have any faith in cops, and neither do our children. It's time to bring up our minds!

> Finally brethren, whatsoever things are true, whatsoever things are honest, whatsoever things are just, whatsoever things are pure, whatsoever things are lovely, whatsoever things are of a good report, if there be any virtue; and if there be any praise, think on these things. *(Phil. 4:8, KJV)*

In the past, our children have patterned themselves after such greats as Martin Luther King Jr. for his tenacity and courage in the civil rights movement, Malcolm X for being venturesome in his pursuit to bring his people together as one body, Michael Jordan for the art and the flare of his aerodynamics, and Magic Johnson for the feats he performed on the basketball courts. We were moved by William Shakespeare, Phillis Wheatley, Edgar Allan Poe, Langston Hughes, Alex Haley, Dr. Maya Angelou, to name a few, for their rhythm, rhyme, and distinctive way with words. We loved Walter Cronkite, Oprah Winfrey, and others like them who have achieved great feats through journalism. We've esteemed Mahalia Jackson, Kirk Franklin, Yolanda Adams, Donnie McClurkin, Leontyne Price, Alvin Ailey Dancers, Lena Horne, Harry Belafonte, Jamie Foxx, Ludwig van Beethoven, Mozart, Miles Davis, Mary J. Blige, Ossie Davis and Ruby Dee, Ciceley Tyson, Denzel Washington, Mel Gibson, Beyonce, Michael Jackson, Whitney Houston, Brandy, and Kriss Kross, for example, for their extraordinary talents in dance, music, and the performing arts. To our little ones, Barney, Strawberry Shortcake, the Care Bears, Bob the Builder, and Elmo are like heroes. There are many more unsung heroes that most of time go unnoticed.

Our children today seem to have chosen role models or idols from the most violent or the most extreme individuals to pattern themselves after. They seem to follow after those who are reprehensible and reprobate in character. They choose to pattern after those who degrade and defame or even those who are very scandalous in behavior, or it's perhaps Hollywood and the world of video games that shapes their lives. They seem to shift and cling to the undesirable elements rather than positive ones. Our children can be like a precious rain forest. Each year we lose more and more of the earth's rain forest to fires, disease, and construction. Our carelessness wipes out the undiscovered inhabitants, rare flowers, herbs (used in medicine to fight disease), and the trees. The end result is less and less rain. If we continue to overlook, ignore, and refuse to pay attention, then like the rain forest we will continue to lose our children until they become almost extinct. By then it may be too late. Let's give them better things and role models to strive for.

There is only One who can truly be considered our most commendable role model. Generations to generations speak of His works. He started out from very lowly, meek, and humble beginnings. He was born in a stable. He had a manger for a bed. At age 12, he showed his ability to teach. He grew up and took over the family's business (preaching the gospel of peace and ministering to needs of others). He worked well with his hands (carpentry). He upheld the laws of the land (a good citizen). He paid taxes (a good steward). He cared about what matters. He was an excellent scholar. He respected his elders. He grew in wisdom, knowledge, and understanding. He had excellent leadership skills. He organized a group of men. He blessed children. He helped the helpless, hopeless, and hapless. He fed the hungry (both naturally and spiritually). He visited the poor. He healed the sick. He restored families. He loved everybody. He was a liberator to those that were bound. He was a peacemaker to those looking for peace.

He could be voted the MVP of a lifetime and all-time MVP (most valuable person). He was a great conversationalist. Boy, could He articulate words! He loved parties (celebrations). He was invited to weddings and dinner parties (e.g., Feast of the Passover). He himself gave a great invitation to life. He was a people person (He was reachable and touchable). Who is this person, you might ask? It's Jesus Christ, the (Messiah) Anointed One, Son of the Living God! He is that friend that sticks closer than a brother, not like the gangs tell you. His love is real and goes deep to everywhere you hurt to bring you healing for your soul, and He is still the same yesterday, today, and forever.

Receive His love. Receive life eternal, He's already paid the price to redeem you, me, and the whole world. Receive Him, and he'll set you free from whatever is binding, hurting, or hindering you!

CHAPTER 6

WHAT IN HELL DO YOU WANT?

During the month of October 2010, the Holy Spirit began discussing heavily with me concerning a matter most urgent and quite disturbing: our final destination. He spoke of the Word, Himself, (Jesus) saying to us words we may not ever want, desire, or long to hear—words of a fate sealed, a final judgment with no hope of ever appealing the sentence. As far as pain goes, this deals with the ultimate rejection, darkness, coldness, vehement heat, and torment unending.

The Lord Jesus gave us a warning from turning from his way. Here the Spirit of the Lord bade me, saying, "Can you wrap your mind around this concept?" The Holy Spirit drove this home quite vividly to me. He painted the picture on the spiritual canvas of my heart. He wanted me to help you get a clear understanding and frame in your mind this message concerning the harvest and winning the lost, and if you are lost, you can come unto repentance and receive the gift of God: eternal life through Christ Jesus.

Lost, according to scripture, means without Christ, without a Shepherd, without being redeemed, without having His blood applied, or being outside of God's fold.

There are many wondrous things in the Word of God that are almost too wonderful to grasp or even think (actually fathom) possible or imaginable. Maybe it's because we really don't view things the way God does. Yet it is because of God's infinite (without limits) wisdom and majesty, versus our being finite (having limits), that he by His Spirit helps us to understand the mighty works of his hands.

> Many, O Lord my God, are thy wonderful works which thou hast done, and thy thoughts which are to us-ward: they cannot be reckoned up in order unto thee: if I would declare and speak of them, they are more than can be numbered. *(Ps. 40:5, KJV)*

Listen to what Job declared to the Lord as he repented:

> ["You asked,] 'Who is this that obscures my counsel without
> knowledge?' Surely I spoke of the things I did not understand,
> things too wonderful for me to know...Therefore I despise myself
> and repent in dust and ashes." *(Job 42:3, 6, KWSB)*

When thinking about the wondrous and fearfully awesome handiwork of God, one must consider his ways pertaining to the aforementioned question. This, by far, is a very pertinent, vitally important, and strikingly alarming question that I or anyone else could be faced to answer. Think about it, are you willing to be honest with yourself? If so, then ask yourself these questions: Am I willing to turn the mirror on myself and face what I see? Am I sitting in the House of God going through the motions Sunday after Sunday, week after, year after year, sliding right into hell? Am I unable to see myself through the eyes of the Lord? If your answer to any of these questions is yes, then ask yourself this: what in hell do I want?

In all honesty, can you actually wrap your mind around going to hell? Think of it, what would anyone want in hell, or why would anyone ever desire to go there? You're probably wondering why is this in this book. It is a very valid thought-provoking question to be considered. Since the Holy Ghost led me to ask this vital self-examining question, I was compelled not only to ask it but also include this eye-opening thought in the book. It may seem a bit rhetorical, utterly absurd, or even a strange thing to ask, but if we are unwilling, stubborn, unforgiving, full of hatred, bitterness, or resentment, if we allow our hurt or pain to cause us to give up and turn our backs on God, then we might just find that we've landed ourselves in hell.

This question deals with where we will spend eternity. There are only two destinations for us: heaven or hell. There are no in-between places; there is no such thing as purgatory. We don't go into limbo either. We aren't reincarnated into an animal or something else, like a supernatural being or even another individual. We don't just die and say that's all to it. We will spend eternity somewhere, whether it is with God in heaven or in the fiery flames and torments of hell, the choice is ours. Here's a bit of truth: we all have an appointment we must keep! Death is the portal to eternity! We all have a date with death. Just as we are born into the world, it is our living that prepares us for—or rather, should prepare us—for dying and life after death.

The scripture says, "And as it is appointed unto men once to die, but after this the judgment" *(Heb. 9:27, KJV)*.

Just as there are two destinations for us to choose from, there are also these:

1. Two ways: the narrow way versus the broad way. One can take you to heaven while the other will land you in hell.

   Enter through the narrow gate, For wide is the gate and broad
   is the road that leads to destruction, and many enter through it.

But small is the gate and narrow the road that leads to life, and only a few find it. *(Matt. 7:13-14, KWSB)*

2. Two deaths: natural death versus spiritual death. One comes at the finish of this life, and the other lasts for all eternity. It is the sleep of the saints versus the second death.

    But the fearful, and unbelieving, and the abominable, and murders, and whoremongers, and sorcerers, and idolaters, and all liars, shall have their part in the lake which burneth with fire and brimstone: which is the second death. *(Rev. 21:8, KJV)*

3. Two resurrections: the rapture or catching away (gathering) of the bride of Christ (His elect, saints) versus the summoning of the lost or those who took the mark of the beast to stand before the great white throne. One leads to everlasting life, the other to eternal death. One gives you eternal joy, the other eternal sorrow.

    And He will send out His angels with a loud trumpet call, and they will gather His elect (His chosen ones) from the four winds, [even] from one end of the universe to the other. *(Matt. 24:31, AMP)*

See also Isaiah 27:13 and Zechariah 9:14.

For the Lord Himself shall descend from heaven with a shout, with the voice of the archangel, and with the trump of God: and the dead in Christ shall rise first: Then we which are alive and remain shall be caught up together with them in clouds, to meet the Lord in the air; and so shall we ever be with the Lord. *(1 Thess. 4:16-17, AMP)*

Nevertheless the solid foundation of God stands, having this seal: "The Lord knows those who are His," and, "Let everyone who names the name of Christ depart from iniquity." *(2 Tim. 2:19, NKJV)*

When Jesus spoke of the kingdom of heaven, he used the dichotomy in the parable of the wheat and the tares, the treasure in the field, and the pearl of great price in this way:

- the sower of the seed = the Son of Man
- the field = the world
- the good seed = the children of the kingdom
- the tares = the children of the wicked one
- the enemy of the tares = the devil

- the harvest = the end of the world
- the reapers = the angels

I will say to the reapers, Gather ye together first the tares, and bind them in bundles to burn them: but gather the wheat into my barn... As therefore the tares are gathered and burned in fire; so shall it be in the end of this world. The Son of man shall send forth his angels, and they shall gather out of his kingdom all things that offend, and them which do iniquity: And cast them into a furnace of fire there shall be wailing and gnashing of teeth. Then shall the righteous shine forth as the sun in the kingdom of their Father. Who hath ears to hear, let him hear...So it will be at the close and consummation of this age. The angels will go forth and separate the wicked from the righteous (those who are upright and in right standing with God) And cast them [the wicked] into the furnace of fire; there will be weeping and wailing and gnashing of teeth. *(Matt. 13:30, 40-43, 49-50, AMP)*

(See also Matt. 24:35-44.)

4. Two judgments: passing before the judgment seat of Jesus versus the great white throne judgment. One seals us to eternal life with the Lord, and the other sentences us to burn perpetually in the lake of fire. Those who receive Jesus as Lord and Savior have life because He is the resurrection and the life. Those who choose not to receive Jesus receives to themselves eternal damnation.

For we shall all stand before the judgment seat of Christ. For it is written, as I live, saith the Lord, every knee shall bow to me, and every tongue shall confess to God. So then every one of us shall give account of himself to God. *(Rom. 14:10-12, KJV)*

For the time is [has arrived] for judgment must begin with the household of God: and if it (first) begin with us, what will [be] the end of those who do not respect or believe or obey the good news (the Gospel) of God? And if the righteous are barely (scarcely) saved, what will become of the godless [ungodly] and wicked [sinner]? *(1 Pet. 4:17-18 AMP; italics added)*

The Lord knoweth how to deliver the godly out of temptations, and to reserve the unjust unto the day of judgment to be punished. *(2 Pet. 2:9, KJV)*

Jesus warns us of the judgment that will befall us all whether we live wholly unto God or contrary to His will.

> When the Son of Man comes in his glory, and all the angels with him, he will sit on his throne in heavenly glory. All the nations will be gathered before him, and he will separate the people one from another as a shepherd separates the sheep from the goats. He will put the sheep on his right and the goats on his left. Then the King will say to those on his right, 'Come, you who are blessed by my Father; *take* your *inheritance*, the kingdom prepared for you since the creation of the world'...Then he will say to those on his left, 'Depart from me, you who are cursed, into the eternal fire prepared for the devil and his angels'.
>
> He will reply, 'I tell you the truth, whatever you did not do for one of the least of these, you did not do for me.' Then they will *go away* to eternal punishment but the righteous to eternal life. *(Matt. 25:31-46, KWSB; italics added)*

5. Two rewards: no more sorrow, grief, pain, or hurt versus the torments of hell. One reward is that we will live forever in God's presence, and in the other, we will live forever with weeping and gnashing of teeth. We'll either be *forever blessed,* abiding continually in God's presence, love, and glory, or *forever cursed* with the full weight of our sins in the flames.

   > For the wages of sin is death; but the gift of God is eternal life through Christ Jesus. *(Rom. 6:23, KJV)*
   >
   > Thou wilt shew me the path of life: in thy presence is fullness of joy; at thy right hand there are pleasures forevermore. *(Ps. 16:11, KJV)*
   >
   > And I heard a great voice out of heaven saying, Behold, the tabernacle of God is with men, and he will dwell with them, and they shall be his people, and God himself shall be with them, and be their God. And God shall wipe away all tears from their eyes; and there shall be no more death, neither sorrow, nor crying, neither shall there be any more pain: for the former things are passed away. *(Rev. 21:3-4, KJV)*

Jesus spoke of the gathering and separating of the children of the kingdom and the children of the wicked one. Throughout Matthew 13, He used parables about the kingdom to give us clarity and understanding of this truth. The Lord Jesus describes what will take place at the close of the age.

So shall it be at the end of the world: the angels shall come forth, and sever the wicked from among just. And shall cast them into the furnace of fire: there shall be wailing and gnashing of teeth. *(Matt. 13:4950, KJV)*

Wrap Your Mind around This!

Can you actually wrap your mind around this concept; "What in hell do you want?" Think of it, what would anyone want in hell or why would anyone desire to go there? You're probably wondering why this is in this book. A very valid thought provoking question to be considered. Since the Holy Spirit led me to ask this vital self-examining question, I was compelled not only to ask; but also include this eye-opening thought in the book. It may seem a bit rhetorical, utterly absurd or a strange thing to ask. But if we are unwilling, stubborn, unforgiving, full of hatred, bitterness or resentment, allowing our hurt or our pain to cause us to give up and turn our backs on God, then we might just find that we've landed ourselves in hell.

There are those who may feel they're already living or have lived in hell, but hell is far more terrifying, dreadful, and horrendous than anyone could ever truly conjure up, fabricate, or imagine. Think about your worst fears being unhampered, running on full blast, set loose, off-the-hook; and running amuck, and even then you still won't come close to the dreadfulness of hell. So you might ask, "What is hell?" or "Is hell really real?" Perhaps you've heard it or even used the explicit term when things didn't go right with you: "What the hell!" Other common expressions are "Who in hell do you think you are?" and the ever-popular phrase "Go to hell!" and "When hell freezes over!" We hear it being used and referred to quite often in movies, sitcoms, and the like, even casually in everyday conversation. Yet hell is a place no one should ever want to go or even see anyone sent to. Did you know that there are some who truly believe that hell is not a physical place. They now teach or preach that it is only a state of mind (because of the hardships, cruelty, situations, or circumstances that we might endure.) So the answer to the question is yes, hell is very real!

Before I define what hell is, let's do a brief recap on what we've discussed so far. We've covered what hurt us, why we're so judgmental, why we hurt, forgiveness, and dealing with our children. This brings us to this point of focus as we look toward having a blessed expected end in Christ Jesus. In the next chapter we'll talk about loss and letting go of our hurt more extensively. We will also deal with separation because of sin and the horrors of facing the ultimate rejection: separated from God for all eternity. Not only does this come from living life without Christ, it also causes us to end up in hell. Hanging on to hurt, anger, fear, lack of faith, and the like will help send us there more swiftly.

Well, what is hell? The scripture states that hell was designed for the devil and his angels (Matt. 25:41). It was never intended for man to go there or reside there. Hell is a dismal, loathsome place otherwise known as Gehenna, Hades, or Sheol, the place of the dead. It is a place where death, pain, punishment, sorrows, and turmoil forever exists, a place of tremendous horrors, like a never-ending nightmare you cannot wake up from, replaying itself over and over again. *Merriam-Webster* defines it as "the realm of the devil" (a misconception, according to scripture) in which the damned suffer everlasting punishment (that's very true, according to scripture).

Jesus described to us the awfulness of hell as he taught about true discipleship in Mark 9:33-48. He shared this after his disciples were disturbed with those who were casting devils out in Jesus' name but were not following them (they were part of the company, just not with the group). Jesus described hell as a place with an unquenchable and inextinguishable fire. It's always hot there. The heat never cools down or goes out, and you cannot put this fire out no matter what you try. It is where the skin worm (maggots) dies not. Jesus said it would be better to be cast into hell missing limbs, feet, eyes, or hands than to be cast in hell with your whole body.

You see, when we find it hard or difficult to trust in the Almighty God and our Father to deliver, set free, and make us whole, then we've underestimated and belittled the wondrous greatness of His love, mercy, grace, power, majesty, glory, and dominion. We dishonor God when we forget it is he that has made us and not we ourselves. We disdain Him when we put our faith in the creature rather than the Creator. There are those who believe there are no absolutes. They don't believe in God or the devil, heaven or hell, the truth or a lie. They believe that there are gray areas. But God is absolutely real! He made heaven, earth, and hell. Whenever we think we know (nobody can tell us otherwise) or think more highly of ourselves than we ought to think or think ourselves to be wise, the Bible says we become fools.

> And he told them this parable; "The ground of a certain rich man *produced a good crop*. He thought to himself, 'What shall I do? I have no place to store my crops.' Then he said, 'This is what I'll do, I will tear down my barns and build bigger ones, and there I will store all my grain and my goods. And I'll say to myself, "You have plenty of good things *laid up* for many years. *Take life easy*; eat, drink and be merry." But God said to him, 'You fool! This very night your life will be *demanded from you*. Then who will get what you have prepared for yourself?' This is how it will be with anyone who *stores up* things for himself but is not rich toward God." *(Luke 12:13-21, KWSB; italics added)*

Here the Lord Jesus warns us against having the spirit of greed or covetousness. In verse 15, Jesus said that a man's life does not consist in the abundance of his possessions. In this parable we see that by having our focus on what we have, what we think we need or want, what we do or have done is the wrong approach, aptitude, and attitude to have in this life, especially if it gives God no glory. The certain rich man represents any of us. Jesus went further to say, "For where your treasure is, there will your heart be also" *(Matt. 6:21, KJV)*. It simply and plainly saying to us that if we're banking on what we possess (our things, talents, gifts, etc.), then we are sadly mistaken. Thus, we've missed God in our unrighteousness, distorted thinking, and wrong motives. We should be like the psalmist and ask the Lord to deliver us from all our transgressions and the reproach of foolishness.

> Lord, make me to know my end, And what is the measure of my days, That I may know how frail I am. Indeed, You have made my days as handbreadths, And my age is as nothing before You; Certainly every man at his best state is but vapor. Selah...And now, Lord, what do I wait for? My hope is in You. Deliver me from all my transgressions; Do not make me the reproach of the foolish. *(Ps. 39:4-8, KJV)*

Watch Your Ways

How we live our lives makes all the difference. Even if we think we're good, all our goodness (good deeds or works) is never good enough to make us good in God's sight. That's why Jesus said, "There is none good, but one, that is God" *(Matt. 19:17, KJV)*. Apostle Paul said, "For we all have sinned and come short of the glory of God" *(Rom. 3:23, KJV)*. On our best day, when we think we're at the top of our game (on top of everything), we can fall dismally short in our ways regarding righteousness and holiness, especially if we are trying to do good or trying to be good without the fruit of His Spirit being evident in our lives. Despite all our efforts to do right, be right, or be in right standing, as the prophet Isaiah said in Isaiah 64:6, "all our righteousness" becomes nothing more than "filthy rags" next to the True Almighty God and his holiness. Without God's divine nature regenerating our nature, we cannot and will not be good.

> You meet and spare him who joyfully works righteousness (uprightness and justice), [earnestly] remembering You in Your ways. Behold, You were angry, for we sinned; we have long continued in our sins [prolonging Your anger]. And shall we be saved? For we have all become like one who is unclean [ceremonially, like a leper], and all our righteousness (our best deeds of rightness and justice) is like filthy rags or a polluted garment; we all fade like a leaf, and our iniquities, like the wind, take us away [far from God's favor, hurrying us toward destruction]. *(Isa. 64:5-6, AMP)*

It takes the blood of Jesus, God's Holy Lamb, to make us clean. We cannot save ourselves and have a need for a Savior. Therefore God prescribed and declared through the prophet Isaiah.

> Learn to do right! Seek justice, relieve the oppressed, and correct the oppressor. Defend the fatherless, plead for the widow. Come now, let us reason together, says the Lord. Though your sins are like scarlet, they shall be white as snow: though they are red like crimson, they shall be like wool. If you are willing and obedient, you shall eat the good of the land. *(Isa. 1:17-19, AMP)*

It takes the righteousness and love of God to help us to display his goodness. Goodness is a part of God. It is a facet (attribute) of the fruit of the Spirit. It is only activated through His love, so in order to be truly good, we must have His Spirit.

> But the fruit of the Spirit is love, joy, peace, longsuffering, gentleness, goodness, faith, Meekness, temperance: against such there is no law. *(Gal. 5:2223, KJV)*

If we are to live victorious, effective, and prosperous lives and win others to Christ, it is imperative we possess the fruit of God's Spirit! That's why we are admonished and instructed to seek after it.

> But seek ye first the kingdom of God, and his righteousness; and all these things shall be added unto you. *(Matt. 6:33, KJV)*

> Beloved, let us love one another: for love is of God; and every one that loveth is born of God, and knoweth God. He that loveth not knoweth not God; for God is love. In this was manifested the love of God toward us, because that God sent his only begotten Son into the world, that we might live through him...No man hath seen God at any time. If we love one another, God dwelleth in us, and his love is perfected in us. *(1 John 4:7-9, 12, KJV)*

Now if we have unbelief that Jesus is who he said he is, then this will cause us to die in our sins and land us right in hell. He warns us against unbelief. Apostle Paul states that we are also defiled when we have an unbelieving heart. Our minds are even polluted, which leads to stinking thinking.

> I said therefore unto you, that ye shall die in your sins: for if ye believe not that I am he, ye shall die in your sins. *(John 8:21, KJV)*

> To the pure all things are pure, but to those who are defiled and unbelieving nothing is pure; but even their mind and conscience are defiled. They profess to know God, but in works they deny Him, and being abominable, disobedient, and disqualified for every good work. *(Titus 1:15-16, NKJV-SSB)*

Jesus is not just a mere man or a prophet. He is the only begotten Son of the Father, God the Son. The Word who is God was God and was with God from the beginning. He is the Living Word made flesh who dwelt among us. He is the bread of life and much, much more! Jesus is the Lamb of Sacrifice who came to take away the sins of the whole world. Jesus is the way!

> For God so loved the world, that he gave his only begotten Son; that whosoever believeth in him should not perish, but have everlasting live. *(John 3:16, KJV)*

> But seek [aim at and strive after] first of all His kingdom and His righteousness [His way of doing and being right], and then all these things taken together will be given you besides. *(Matt. 6:33, AMP)*

Review these two lists below. Are there any of these things that could send you to hell in your life or part of your lifestyle? Did you find yourself on the side that sends us to hell or on the side that keeps us out of it? If so, then surrender them and yourself to the Lord Jesus.

What Can Send Us to Hell Versus What Keeps Us Out

Unforgiveness	Forgiveness
Unbelief	Belief that God is the Lord
Pride; God resists the proud	Humility; God gives grace to the humble
Greed	A cheerful giver; God loves
Lust; brings forth sin	Love never fails
Being a liar	Being honest, faithful, and true
Rebellion; God rejects	Submission; draws God near
Idolatry; worshipping things	True worshiper; worships God only
Disobedience	Obedience; follows God with all
Works of the flesh	Having the fruit of the Spirit
Proud look.; God hates	A broken heart and a contrite spirit
Blaspheming the Holy Spirit	Being led by the Holy Spirit
Loving the world	Loving the Lord
Faithlessness	Having faith in God
Walking in darkness	Walking in the Spirit
Being children of darkness	Being children/heirs of God
Having your Way	Following God's way
Hardness of Heart	Repentance
Continuing in sin	Being redeemed
Being counterfeit	Being a true disciple/believer
Yielding to sin	Surrendering to Jesus Christ

Sin-stained and blemished	Washed in the blood of the Lamb
Rejecting God	Receiving Jesus as Lord and Savior
The mark of the beast	Sealed by the Spirit of God

Take a look at the certain rich man and Lazarus, a certain beggar who lay at the rich man's gate. The rich man was arrayed (dressed) in purple and fine linen. He feasted and made merry in splendor (luxury) every day. Lazarus was full of (ulcerated) sores. He desired the crumbs from the rich man's table. Jesus said that the dogs had more compassion on Lazarus than the rich man because they licked his sores. The rich man lived a life of self-gratification and leisure instead of a life of service, appreciation, and regard for God and his fellow man. He didn't love his neighbor as himself. He only loved himself. He was caught having delusions of grandeur. Remember, this could be you!

> And it came to pass, that the beggar died, a and was carried by the angels into Abraham's bosom: the rich man also died, and was buried; And in hell he *lift up his eyes*, being *in torments* [agony], and seeth Abraham afar off, and Lazarus in his bosom. And he cried and said, Father Abraham, have mercy on me, and send Lazarus, that he may dip the tip of his finger in water, and cool my tongue; for I am *tormented in this flame*. But Abraham said, Son, remember that thou in thy lifetime receivedst thy good things [comforts and delights], and Lazarus evil things [discomforts and distress]: but now he is comforted; and thou art tormented. And beside all this, between us and you there is a *great gulf fixed*: so that they which would pass from hence to you cannot; neither can they pass to us, that would come from thence. *(Luke 16:19-31, KJV; italics added)*

The rich man found himself in a place of great sorrow, anguish, grief, and pain. The prophet Isaiah said that hell had enlarged itself. Perhaps the rich man's motto in life was like Burger King's slogan "Have it your way" or the Isley Brothers' song *It's Your Thing*. It speaks about self-gratification, doing whatever with whomever, however, and wherever you so choose. It's a careless, callous, casual affair with no real commitment, devotion, or concern about the individuals involved, and it also somewhat reprimands the woman for her actions when she was told "do what you want to do, I don't care." It's like this: if it feels good to you, then do it. May God help us not to be so disconcerting.

> It's your thing, do what you wanna do.
> I can't tell you, who to sock it to.
> It's your thing, do what you wanna do.
> I can't tell you, who to sock it to.

If you want me to love you, maybe I will.
Believe me woman, it ain't no big deal.
You need love now, just as bad as I do.
Make's me no difference now, who you give your thing to.

I'm not trying to run your life, I know you wanna do what's right.
Give your love now, to whoever you choose.
How can you love, with the stuff you use now.

The rich man perhaps didn't believe, had no clue, or didn't realize or even imagine that his ways or lifestyle would cause him to end up in hell. His ways might have been pleasing to him, but they were not to God. He definitely missed God with the stuff he used. In verses 27-31, he tried to convince Abraham to send him to his father's house so he could warn his five brothers to change their ways so that they wouldn't also end up in hell. Abraham told him that they had Moses and the prophets to heed. The rich man wanted to beg the difference. He told Abraham No; but relayed that if someone came from the dead to warn them, that maybe then they would repent. (It would appear he didn't get the message: there is no exit out of hell!) Abraham told him if they wouldn't hear Moses and the prophets and repent, they certainly wouldn't be persuaded by one who rose from the dead. What a tragedy, to live a life of comfort or ease, a good life, only to die and open your eyes in the torments of hell!

Let Jesus be Lord of your life.
Don't try to have it your way. It won't end well.

> There is a way which seemth right unto a man, but the end
> thereof are the ways of death. *(Prov. 14:12, KJV)*

I once saw an illustration (http://www.theinterviewwithgod.com) called "An Interview with God." There was one question asked that stood out to me (I adjure you, examine closely the reply):

"What surprises You most about humankind?"
God answered; "They get bored with childhood.
Rush to grow up, and then long to be children again."
"That they loose their health to make money, and
then lose their money to restore their health."
"That by thinking anxiously about the future, they forget the
present, such that they live in neither the present nor the future."

"That they live as if they will never die, and die as though they
had never lived."

Could you see yourself in this interview? This stood out to me because we actually see this played out every day.

Did you realize that there are those who aren't even sure what they believe in or in whom they serve? What about those who are curious about other religions and doctrines? Some would even dare venture to dabble in witchcraft looking for the answers to their questions yet never finding them. There are also those who will try to circumvent God's way to suit their needs. Like the scripture says, "Having a form of godliness, but denying the power thereof" *(2 Tim. 3:5, KJV)*. Titus 1:16 also says, "They profess to know God [to recognize, perceive, and be acquainted with Him], but deny *and* disown and renounce Him by what they do, they are detestable, *and* loathsome, unbelieving *and* disobedient and disloyal *and* rebellious, and [they are] unfit *and* worthless for good work (deed or enterprise) of any kind." We try to live our lives (carry out our agendas) first, then if we have the time or remember, we may choose to give God some of it. This is the wrong position to take.

Putting to Bed the Myths

Let's dispel some myths about hell:

1. I'll see all my friends in hell.

   Hell is not user- or people-friendly. It's full of despicable, distressing horrors beyond description. You won't be able or even want to hook up with your homeys, buddies, family members, or friends. If you do run across them, you'll probably be angry they didn't warn you not to go there.

2. Going to hell will be a piece of cake compare to this.

   Some think a stint (stay) in hell will be easy-peasy or a cakewalk compared to whatever state they've lived or are living in. Such is their mind-set. But in hell They don't leave the light on for you like the Super 8 Motel. There isn't a welcome mat put out for you. There are no amenities or plush accommodations either. If you go there, you'll probably try to find the nearest exit, and there is none!

3. When we get to hell we can party all the time.

   You won't find any parties going on in hell. There won't be anything to celebrate there. Instead of being at the marriage feast of the Lamb, you'll be engulfed in sorrows and torments of hell's fiery flames. There will be *nothing* but weeping and wailing and gnashing of teeth!

4. I won't be lonely in hell.

Hell is a place where everyone is alone to suffer in agony for eternity. You probably be looking for someone or some way to get comfort and ease from your torment, but in this place there is no such thing as comfort, company, or care.

5. If I die, I can repent and God will save me.

    If we die in our sins, like the rich man in hell, we will lift up our eyes. There's no guarantee that you will even have time to repent as the breath of life is leaving your body or that that will be your response or final thought.

    The scripture says, "For without the shedding of blood there is no remission [pardon of sin]" *(Heb. 9:22, KJV)*.

    Unless the blood of Jesus, God's sacrificial Lamb for our atonement, has been applied to our lives, our sins will be imputed to us. We will pay the penalty of sin, death, especially if we neglect, refuse, or reject God's wonderful gift of life.

    Remember what Hebrews 9:27 (KJV) says about our appointment with death and judgment: "And as it is appointed unto men once to die, but after this the judgment." This is the one appointment we all must keep.

6. God is a loving God. He would never send anyone to hell.

    Jesus said that God is able to cast the body and soul into hell. He told us not to fear what man can do to us more than what God will do when we fail to love, obey, honor, and serve Him.

    And do not be afraid of those who kill the body but cannot kill the soul: but rather be afraid of Him who can destroy both soul and body in hell (Gehenna). *(Matt. 10:28, AMP)*

    Though God is a loving God and is love, He is also just. Therefore the scripture says,

    And he [God] passed in front of Moses, proclaiming, "The Lord, the Lord, the compassionate and gracious God, slow to anger, abounding in love and faithfulness, maintaining love to thousands, and forgiving wickedness, rebellion and sin. Yet he does not leave the guilty unpunished." *(Exod. 34:6-7, KWSB)*

    For if God spared not the angels that sinned, but cast them down to hell, and delivered them into chains of darkness, to be reserved unto judgment. *(2 Pet. 2:4, KJV)*

King David speaks of the ways of the wicked, stating it is not God but the wicked who causes the wrath of God to fall upon them, making their final resting place hell.

The Lord is known by the judgment which he executeth: the wicked is snared in the work of his own hands, Higgaion. Selah (pause; chew on that). The wicked shall be turned into hell, and all the nations that forget God. *(Ps. 9:16-17, KJV)*

Because God made us free moral agents and beings of choice, we can make the conscious decision whether to live holy or to live wickedly, whether to be a sinner or be saved by His grace, whether to be lost or be redeemed by the blood of His Lamb, Christ Jesus, but if we choose to live wickedly, we should know that just as the scripture has said, we will end up in hell.

7. There are many ways to get to heaven.

On the contrary, there is but one way: Jesus Christ the Son of the Living God!

Jesus saith unto him. I am the way, the truth and the life: no man cometh unto the Father, but by me. *(John 14:6 KJV)*

Jesus taught about the two gates and paths that we can choose from—the narrow and wide gates. One leads to life while the other leads to destruction, which I touched on earlier when speaking of the two ways *(Matt. 7:13-14).*

We cannot get to God and heaven any other way but through Jesus, the door! We cannot expect to get there unless we come in by the Lord Jesus! And if we try to enter in another way, Jesus said that we are nothing but thieves and robbers.

I am the Door: anyone who enters in through Me will be saved (will live). He will come in and he will go out [freely], and will find pasture. *(John 10:9, AMP)*

Hell, the Place of No Escape!

Hollywood's film industry made a horror/suspense movie series called *The Final Destination.* Each episode is filled with more thrills and horrors, each being far more grotesque than the previous one. This film series was made to keep you at the edge of your seat until the final blow of death was given. The basis of these films featured a victim/hero having premonitions about the impending deaths of his friends and loved ones. He would try to help keep them alive all while trying to avoid dying himself. The way the plot of the movies ran, as though death was and is final, gives the false hope that depicted we could cheat death or stop it somehow. The time line in the movies stretched over a ten-year period, with people dying horrific deaths. Although these movies have a strong violent content with gruesome accidents, they only deal with dying. But death is not the final destination. Like I mentioned earlier, death is the portal to eternity.

Death only becomes our final destination when we die in our sins and go to hell. It is where one would want to die and desire that that was all to it, but hurriedly and precipitately we will find that hell was and is filled with fearsome dread. It's final if you're unfortunate to be one of the ones who will have to stand before the great white throne judgment. It's final if your name is not found in the Book of Life, and when you're finished there, you'll then immediately be given over to burn forever in the lake of fire. That's more eerie, awful, dreadful, horrific, gruesome, frightening, and terrifying than anything Hollywood can ever dream up, imagine, fantasize about, or create concerning death, hell, or the grave.

> And death and hell were cast into the lake of fire. This is the
> second death. And whosoever was not found written in the book
> of life was cast into the lake of fire. *(Rev. 20:14-15, KJV)*

Pastor John Hagee has a film out called *Escape from Hell*. This film is being used as a ministry tool to help reach the lost. Its objective is to try and turn many out the broad way back to the narrow way, which is in Christ Jesus. Though the depiction is astounding and quite revealing, believe this, many will still take it for granted, but going to hell is no laughing matter! The truth of the matter is in hell there will be no escape from your deepest and greatest fear running away with you. Anxiety will be without a buffer, and there will be nothing to calm you down. Your senses will be in overdrive. There will be no place of peace or rest, no end to the fierce onslaught of torments there. You'll experience fear on a level that's truly out of this world! No filmmaker has ever or can truly prepare you for the overwhelming sorrows of hell, even in their wildest imagination. There'll be no escape once you get there!

Perhaps it is because of what Hollywood and our own efforts have shown us that we believe this way? Is this why we've become a people so desensitized, degraded, and demoralized that we're lulled into believing that the devil is some fictitious character with horns and a pitchfork? God help us! We've been led to believe that the devil rules over hell or that he doesn't even exist. Maybe we also want to believe or accept that hell isn't real either. On the contrary, the devil is very real and doesn't rule over hell. According to the Word of God, hell was made for him (the devil) and his angels. Hell is a prison facility unlike any other. As the old folks would say "Quiet as it's kept," the devil will also be thrown into hell. His days are numbered. And after this judgment known as the second death, the devil, all those whose names were not found in the book of life, all those who forget God (I'm talking about the True and Living God who was, who is, and is to come), hell, and the grave will be cast into the lake of fire.

Will you be found in this place? Are you living to die, to be cast into hell, then be resurrected, judged, and sentenced only to die again the second time, this time without end? If you're sinning, you're not winning or gaining eternal life.

Here's the concept the Holy Spirit showed me: walk with me in your mind's eye for a moment.

Suppose you died (God forbid), and you found yourself standing before the judgment seat of the Lord, and the books were opened, as well as the book of life. As you stand there, you virtually see your life flash before your face. Stunned, you probably think this all a dream. There is no way this could actually be happening, but at that very moment you would find that this is really taking place. Perhaps you thought you lived a pretty decent and comfortable life. You didn't offend anyone. You tried to get along with everybody. You said you were a Christian, though you never shared your faith with anyone. You never had the time. You were only a Christian when you wanted to be (fronting and flogging). You were dressing the part and confessing but barely practicing what you were professing. You said you tried to live the best you knew how. Instead of you persuading and converting others to Christ, they persuaded you. Not realizing you've denied Christ before others, now He will deny you before His Father.

> But whosoever shall deny me before men, him will I also deny before my Father which is in heaven. *(Matt. 10:33, KJV)*

Maybe you lived a life of unbelief (you didn't trust God or take Him at his word), or you had a form of godliness (you went to church regularly, watched church on TV, or something like that), but denied the power of God. You worshiped the Lord with your lips, but your heart was far from it (meaning, you were focused on something other than God). Could it be that you died abruptly without the chance to surrender your life to Christ? Whatever the case, here you stand without a priest, without a preacher, without your mom or dad, without your BFF (best friend forever), or the like, just you, alone before the Lord and his judgment council. Except in this court, judgment is final. There are no pardons, no grace period, no appeals of the sentence, no retrials, no getting off for good behavior, and did I mention? Sentencing is expeditiously carried out: post haste!

Here's what you would have to look forward to after sentencing:

1. You will have to deal with these words: "Depart from me." That's the ultimate rejection, the ultimate separation for all time.

2. Then you are cast out into darkness—void of light, void of warmth, void of God's love and presence. (You probably are still reeling from having to hear Jesus say, "Depart from me. I never knew you." It will play over and over and over again in your head. It will be a never-ending replay from that moment

on, before you could ever begin to deal with the darkness.) Have you absorbed it yet?

3. Next you will find yourself burning, yet not burning up, for all eternity in the lake of fire.

4. And just when you thought you've experienced the worst, you find yourself in total anguish that has overtaken your senses because you're being eaten by skin worms and you cannot get away from the foul stench of rotting, burning flesh. Imagine fiery agony, you cannot begin to conceive its magnitude. And if it could be based or measured on the Richter scale, the adrenaline rush, the fear, and everything you felt would be literally off the charts!

5. Then you face the torment of no peace. You look for rest but find none.

6. You have no way to get relief. There's no water or cooling system in hell or the lake of fire. Your sweat won't even cool you off.

7. You will experience being able to look up, seeing where you could have been, but will never ever be able to go there. You will see your loved ones and others but will be unable to get their attention. They will not heed your pleas for help.

Dejected, separated, alone in the darkness, your only company is skin worms, fear, panic, unrest, a hurt and sorrow unending, and fierce fiery flames that cannot be put out.

> There will be weeping and grinding of teeth when you see Abraham and Isaac and Jacob and all the prophets in the kingdom of God, but you yourselves being cast forth [banished, driven away]. *(Luke 13:28, AMP)*

Now tell me, can you wrap your mind around this concept? What in Hell do you want?

A Word of Caution

Accept the Lord Jesus as your Savior, Healer, and Redeemer! Serve, trust, and love Him with your all! For if today you reject Him and you choose not to receive his gift of life, on the day that you die, please don't be surprised for you will surely find yourself in the place made for the devil and his angels, a place full of great sorrow, torment, and pain, your freedom never to regain.

So please believe this will be your reality if heaven is not your final destination and Jesus does not reign in your life. Do not make the mistake of dismissing this message or casting it to the side. For if you deny Jesus, your name won't be written in the book of life.

Then, my friend, prepare your heart to hear Jesus say, "Depart from me. I know you not!" And at once He will send you away. It will be too late then to receive His love for you, too late to give your heart to Him, too late to love God and fellow man, too late to partake of the blessing and not the curse, too late to have life and not death, too late to be a witness and share the good news and glad tidings with others, too late to reach out and win a lost sister or brother, too late to repent for your sins and gain eternal life with Him. It will be too late, I tell you, much too late then. And for certain, just like the rich man, in hell you will lift up your eyes!

CHAPTER 7

LET IT GO

The Lord gave and the Lord hath taken away: blessed be the
name of the Lord.

—*Job 1:21 (KJV)*

What is loss but the things that we ourselves must at times let go, things that sometimes we hold on to so dearly it seems it is with our very soul. Loss plays an important part of life, important in its building as it opens up our eyes. It opens our emotions through our suffering, grief, and pain. Loss teaches us lessons (if we choose to learn from it) and the values of living, giving, loving, and how to remain so. It may seem it has no real value or benefit, but it draws us closer despite our differences. It demonstrates to us that we should not compete with one another but rather walk together with love. Loss knows no color, race, ethnicity, or creed. Loss has no boundaries, except when it comes to the Lord Jesus Christ! Apostle Paul reassured us with this when our lives are lost in Jesus:

> So then, we are always full of good and hopeful and confident courage; we know that while we are at home in the body, we are abroad from the home with the Lord [that is promised us]...[Yes] we have confident hopeful courage and are pleased rather to be away from home out of the body and be at home with the Lord. Therefore, whether we are at home [on earth away from Him] or away from home [and with Him], we are constantly ambitious and strive earnestly to be pleasing to Him. *(2 Cor. 5:6, 8-9, AMP)*

Loss can be destructive when we are not willing to let go (surrender). Loss can be from the pain of separation. Sometimes separation can be because of sin in our lives. Throughout the Bible we are given multiple examples of this separation: Adam and Eve in Genesis 3:8, the wheat and the tares in Matthew 13:1-43, and the parables of the ten virgins in Matthew 25:1-13 and the prodigal son in Luke 15:11-32, to name a few. Sin separates us from God. Jesus warns us about this separation when he said,

> Loss n I: the state or fact of being destroyed: RUIN 2: the harm resulting from losing 3: something that is lost 4pl: killed, wounded or captured soldiers 5: failure to win 6: an amount by which the cost exceeds the selling price 7: decrease in amount or degree 8: the act of losing possession — 5.1

> Not every one that saith unto me, Lord, Lord, shall enter into the kingdom of heaven; but he that doeth the will of my Father which is in heaven. And then will I profess unto them, I never knew you: depart from me, ye that work iniquity. *(Matt. 7:21, 23, KJV)*

This will be the ultimate rejection—the loss of the light of the Lord, the loss of His eternal warmth, the loss of His everlasting love, the loss of His presence not just for a moment or a day or a year but for all eternity, time without end. (I explained this in greater detail in the previous chapter). This is not where any of us should desire to be. We should draw closer to God and strengthen our relationship with Him. The apostle Paul challenges us not to let anything or anyone separate us from the love of God.

> Separate vb rated; • rat-ing I: to set or keep apart: DISCONNECT 2: to keep apart by something intervening 3: to cease Io be together: PART adj 4: existing by itself 5: not shared with another: breakup. dissociate, disunite, dissolve, divorce, resolve, sever, unyoke - 5.2

> Who shall ever separate us from Christ love? Shall suffering and affliction and tribulation? Or calamity and distress? Or persecution or hunger or destitution or peril or sword? Even as it is written, For Thy sake we are put to death all the day long; we are regarded and counted as sheep for the slaughter. Yet amid all these things we are more than conquerors and gain a surprising victory through Him Who loved us. For I am persuaded beyond doubt [am sure] that neither death nor life, nor angels nor principalities, nor things impending and threatening nor things to come, nor powers, Nor height nor depth, nor anything else in all creation will be able to separate us from the love of God which is in Christ Jesus our Lord. *(Rom. 8:35-39, AMP)*

(See also Ps. 44:22.)

Don't let *anything* separate you from God! Not even yourself!

Repentance—Letting Go God's Way

Being broken is the first step to repentance. It is through our brokenness that God's healing and atoning word can be implemented at the very point of our hurt. As long as we resist Him, we prolong the agony and hold back the relief He has for us. He comes to apply the ointment (oil) that will cure our wound.

> The Lord is near to those who have a broken heart, and saves such as have a contrite spirit. *(Ps. 34:18, NKJV-SSB)*

But what, you may ask, is repentance? And how does it help us to let go?

> *Repentance* is contrition for sin, the action or process of repenting esp. for misdeeds or moral shortcomings.

> *Repent* — change mind, purpose. 1: to turn from sin and resolve to reform one's life 2: to feel sorry for *(something done):* REGRET (http://dictionary.com/, Merriam-Webster's Dictionary)

In 2 Chronicles 7:14 (KJV), the Lord God gave a call of repentance to his people.

> If My people, which are called by my name, shall humble themselves, and pray, and seek my face, and turn from their wicked way; then will I hear from heaven, and will forgive their sin, and will heal their land.

This call was not to the world (sinners, those who did not know God), but to those who were of the household of faith. It was not unlike the call He gave to the prophet Isaiah to come to Him and be cleansed (Isa. 1:18-20). It was to those who said they believed His name yet were missing the mark. It was a call back to holiness because God is holy. If we want to reap the benefits God has for us, we must be willing to submit ourselves to Him and his ways. We must be willing to obey Him emphatically with our whole heart. If we love God like we say we do, then we will be willing to turn from whatever it may be and leave it behind (on the altar of sacrifice, at the foot of the cross) that we may follow him.

The Lord gave us specific directions for repentance as his people and children. Let's review them:

1. We must humble ourselves. God gives grace to the humble. His word declares that he resist, oppose, fight, and withstand the proud. God will esteem, lift up, or promote those who are of a humble state. Humbling ourselves before God as little children to their Father gives us access to his kingdom.

And whosoever shall exalt himself shall be abased; and he that shall humble himself shall be exalted. *(Matt. 23:12,)*

Whoever humble himself therefore and become like this little child [trusting, lowly, loving, forgiving] is the greatest in the kingdom of heaven. *(Matt. 18:4, AMP)*

2. We must pray. We must not only rely on someone else praying for you only, but you must open your own mouth and pray. And when we pray we must believe! This is illustrated in the parable of the unjust judge found in Luke 18:1-8.

    And he spoke a parable unto them to this end, that men ought always to pray, and not faint.

    We are urged in the first letter to the church at Thessalonica to pray *without ceasing (1 Thess. 5:17)*. We must also pray in faith!

3. We must seek His face. Often we seek God's hand. We want the blessing but seem to reject the Blesser. That will not work! As in the passage in 2 Chronicles 7, the Lord God seeks to be sought after. Jesus said that Father seeks those who will worship Him in spirit and in truth.

    I love them that love me; and those that seek me early shall find me. *(Prov. 8:17, KJV)*

    And ye shall seek me, when ye shall search for me with all your heart. And I will be found of you, saith the Lord: and I will turn away your captivity. *(Jer. 29:13-14, KJV)*

    David gave Solomon these instructions about seeking God:

    And you, Solomon my son, know the God of your father [have personal knowledge of Him, be acquainted with, and understand Him; appreciate, heed, and cherish Him] and serve Him with a blameless heart and a willing mind. For the Lord searches all hearts and minds and understands all wanderings of the thoughts. If you seek Him [inquiring for and of Him and requiring Him as your first and vital necessity] you will find Him; but if you forsake Him, He will cast you off forever. *(1 Chron. 28:9, AMP)*

4. We must turn! We cannot stay where we are if we want God's favor, forgiveness, restoration, provision; and grace. If we choose not to turn to God; we forfeit the blessing of his love,

mercy and favor. We must meet God on his terms. We must answer His call and come!

> Come now, and let us reason together, saith the Lord: though your sins be as scarlet, they shall be as white as snow: though they be red like crimson, they shall be as wool. If ye be willing and obedient, ye shall eat the good of the land: But if ye refuse and rebel, ye shall be devoured with the sword: for the mouth of the Lord hath spoken it. *(Isa. 1:18-20, KJV)*

Serving the Lord requires active participation from you!

This was also demonstrated in the scriptures where after Jesus healed the man who was sick of the palsy, the Pharisees questioned his disciples concerning the matter, not fully understanding what had taken place. They thought He was wrong for eating with the publicans and sinners. They questioned His authority. They questioned Him, not realizing that Jesus was the Good Physician (Yahweh-Rapha: Jehovah Rapha), the Redeemer from sin.

> For I am the Lord that healeth thee. *(Exod. 15:26, KJV)*

Jesus' reply was that of mercy and grace extended to those who needed to be healed. Through Christ, repentance brings healing.

> They that be whole need not a physician, but they that are sick. But go ye and learn what that meaneth, I will have mercy, and not sacrifice; for I am not come to call the righteous, but sinners to repentance. *(Matt. 9:12-13, KJV)*

In the Old Testament, we find many examples, shadows, or types of God's forgiveness, the efforts, and ways redemption was to be carried out to make one clean. Because God is holy, we who are his people, his children, must also be holy. Our redemption was built or founded on something more precious than the blood of goats, bullocks, and turtledoves. It is founded on and in the blood of Jesus! It is the universal and eternal remedy for all that ails us and makes us sick. We become justified through Christ because God is the Justifier.

> For all have sinned, and come short of the glory of God; Being justified freely by His grace through the redemption that is in Christ Jesus: Whom God hath set forth to be a propitiation through faith in his blood, to declare his righteousness for the remission of sins that are past, through the forbearance of God;
>
> To declare, I say, at this time his righteousness: that he might be just, and the justifier of him which believeth in Jesus. *(Rom. 3:23-26, KJV)*

Simply going to God and repenting opens up for us the well of salvation where we can drink deeply of the rivers of life. Repentance brings us to the heart of God. It restores us to the right place with Him. If we refuse to change, refuse to turn, then we will remain guilty as charged. We will remain outside of grace, which has already been given through the redemptive work of Jesus Christ. A repentant heart is a must. As I stated previously, David wrote that he would not hold or hide iniquity in his heart. He did not want to be shut out of God's presence. He did not want to lose God's precious Spirit in his life. He learned that holding on to things and not letting them go was not trusting in God.

One of the greatest psalms David wrote, Psalms 51, dealt with his repentance when the prophet Nathan came to him after he had gone to Bathsheba and had Uriah, her husband, killed. David cried out to God for his mercy, appealing to the Lord's loving-kindness and tender mercies. He ask God to blot out his transgressions and to cleanse him. David implored the Lord to wash him thoroughly. He admitted to God that he sinned against Him only and did evil in His sight. David asked God to purge him, take away all his iniquities (wrongdoings), give him a clean heart, and renew a right spirit within. He didn't want the Lord to turn him away or to remove His Holy Spirit from him. He pleaded with God to restore the joy of His salvation. He wanted to be delivered from bloodguiltiness. David knew that it took real brokenness of the spirit and a contrite heart (remorseful, penitent, repentant) to humbly and thoroughly surrender (yield) to God. He knew that the only sacrifice that would be acceptable unto God would be the sacrifice of a broken spirit. This is what it means to have godly sorrow.

When Shall I Let Go?

It is regretful, deplorable, poignant, even distressful to continue holding on to something, like an awful occurrence, that has long passed. Even when God has removed or is trying to remove those things from our lives, we tend to want to hold on to them and not let go. Letting go of our past hurts and pains will not only defuse it (render it powerless) but also subdue (to vanquish) it. You regain dominion in that area of life. Constantly, incessantly, invariably reliving it in our heart, mind, soul, and spirit is simply ludicrous. Whatever you're delivered, released, and set free from becomes your greatest tool of witness, your testimony. In Revelation 12:11 (KJV), the scripture says, "And they overcame him by the blood of the Lamb, and by the word of their TESTIMONY; and they loved not their lives unto the death."

You've got to know the greater One is in you.

> Ye are of God, little children, and have overcome them: because
> GREATER is he that is in you, than he that is in the world.
> *(1 John 4:4, SPLB)*

So whatever it is you need to let go of, let go and let God!

Let's look at how the prophet in Isaiah 6:1-8 dealt with being rent, separated, and set apart from King Uzziah. Sometimes we cannot see the glory that lies ahead because we are focused in (stuck on) or are too close to the situation, circumstance, or event. The moment the prophet Isaiah began to deal with the death of King Uzziah, he was able to see clearly the glory and majesty of the true King: God. Isaiah saw the holiness of the Lord God. He realized his self-worth. He could see who God was and where he really stood before him. He let go of any falsehoods or pretentious thoughts he might've had about himself, life—the whole enchilada, to coin a phrase. He let go of anything and anyone who could forfeit his future. He let go of himself to the True and Living God. And so should we.

Do you have any Uzziahs or anything you need to let go to God that may be hindering you or has you so transfixed you can't move forward? Or is there something that keeps you from being obedient and walking in God's perfect will?

If so, then turn it over to the Lord's hand and provisional care. Let God arise in you. Let God heal and mend your every wound.

Remember Job in chapter 1 "What Hurt Us"? He was a significantly wealthy and righteous (upright) man. He suffered loss economically: His cattle (livestock)—five hundred yoke of oxen and five hundred donkeys—were carried away by the Sabeans, his seven thousand sheep and servants consumed by fire from the sky, his three thousand camels taken away by the Chaldeans. He lost his entire staff; his servants were killed by the sword. Job even suffered the loss of his seven sons and three daughters. All this transpired in one day. He suffered loss in cataclysmic proportions not over a process of time but all in one day. It didn't come quietly with regard to Job's temperament or whether his heart could withstand it. His loss came suddenly and fiercely and without any warning. Before he had time to adjust from the first blow, he was hit with another one and then another one and so on. My God, what a shocker that had to have been!

After receiving these chronicles of bad news, the scripture say this:

> Then Job arose and rent his mantle, and shaved his head, and fell down upon the ground and worshipped. And said, Naked came I out of my mother's womb, and naked shall I return thither: the Lord gave, and the Lord hath taken away; blessed be the name of the Lord. In all this Job sinned not, nor charged God foolishly. *(Job 1:20-22, KJV)*

He didn't blame God for the series of unfortunate events that were taking place in his life. He definitely proved Satan to be a liar.

Yet his loss didn't end there. He was relinquished of his health, covered from head to toe by oozing painful boils, using a piece of broken potsherd to scrape himself. He suffered loss socially; his friends deserted and dejected him. His wife told him to curse God and die, to give up because everything they had was gone. He was literally stripped down to nothing.

After going through a period of sounding out, Job had this resolve:

> For I know that my redeemer liveth, and that he shall stand at the latter day upon the earth; And though after my skin worms destroy this body, yet in my flesh shall I see God. *(Job 19:25-26, KJV)*

Job's confidence was not in himself but in God to deliver him.

In the introduction, I talked about the loss of my fiancé and how it caused or brought up the hurt of my past, those things that I thought I was healed from. I found myself in an avalanche of hurt. It seemed I was being crushed by the pain of separation, heartbreak, and the need for closure. I was crushed from the pain of being raped both physically and spiritually, crushed from the pain of verbal and mental abuse, rejection, and the feeling of abandonment. It seemed I was being crushed on all sides. It wasn't until I was willing to let go of what I couldn't change (I couldn't bring Karlton back) did the healing process begin. If I was to move forward and help my children deal with his death, I had to trust God with my heart, mind, and spirit. Before I could reach out to them, I had to reach up and out. I had to do it the way the Holy Spirit was instructing me to do it. The wall I had enclosed myself in had to come down. That's when I found that God was there all the time, just waiting to heal and restore me.

The Lord extended me a lifeline. I grabbed hold of it for dear life. It came when I was shutting everyone out, both male and female. I didn't care to be bothered with people. I just wanted the dagger in my heart to be removed. That's when the Holy Spirit directed me to reach out. God sent someone to help me even though I was reluctant to receive the help He sent. It was like what the Lord Jesus told Saul on the road to Damascus: "It's hard to kick against the prick." (And boy, was I kicking against it, not realizing I was hurting myself). It was only when I let it all go to the Lord that I benefited from the help he gave. Today, I am truly grateful God extended his mercy to me. At that moment I realized the Lord reached out to restore me.

If you're trying to rescue someone who's drowning, and they're fighting, kicking, struggling to save themselves, there's the possibility that both of you will drown, but if you can get them to stop panicking and being overwhelmed with the situation, to calm down and trust in their rescuer to help them, then and only then can the assistance you offer be received without detrimental consequences, ensuring that both of you will live.

In Job 42:10 (KJV), we see God moved on his behalf.

> And the Lord turned the captivity of Job, when he prayed for his friends: also the Lord gave Job twice as much as he had before.

He received double for his trouble when he prayed not for himself but for his friends! When he truly let go, he saw the hand of God move greater for him than before. God flipped the script! God turned a bad situation around for his good. (Read the book of Job.) Won't you let go of all that may be or is holding you hostage today and allow Christ to come and have his way? We conquer the devil our adversary when we let go, and because Christ overcame the world, we too can overcome. Here's your backup:

> These things I have spoken unto you, that in me ye might have peace: In this world ye shall have tribulation: but be of good cheer; I have overcome the world. *(John 16:33, KJV)*

> And we know that all things work together for good to them that love God, to them who are the called according to his purpose. For whom he did foreknow, he also did predestinate to be conformed to the image of his Son, that the might be the firstborn among many brethren. Moreover whom he did predestinate them he also called: and whom he called, them he also justified: and whom he justified, them he also glorified... Nay, in all these things we are more than conquerors through him that loved us. *(Rom. 8:2830, 37, KJV)*

> For whatsoever is born of God overcometh the world: and this is the victory that overcometh the world, even our faith. *(1 John 5:4, KJV)*

Let it out. Let it go. Give it up! And don't pick it up anymore!

Here's a word of encouragement:

Let go of yesterday's past. Weep no more. It's time to laugh. A merry heart works like good medicine. Let go to a glad heart. Take hold of a new day. Catch a glimpse of a brand-new start. Let go of those embers of your losses. Let go to see the glory of the Lord in your life begin to shine. Loss does not mean the end to everything. In itself loss brings about a beginning when some things come to an end. Newness begins when Christ has taken up full reins of your soul. In Luke 9:23-26, we are admonished by our Lord Jesus Christ to let go or turn over our lives to his care. If we try to save it, we'll lose it, and if we'll lose our lives (ourselves) in Him, we'll gain eternal life. By disowning (denying) self and taking up our cross daily and following Him, we are assured of life abundantly through him. That's when we can say within ourselves, "I shall to Him let go."

What is lost to us many times we find again. What is taken from us many times we build again. What is rent from us we always seem to mend. When we look beneath the underlying pain, we can always see the healing in His wings. What we sow we know that we shall reap in time. What we give away we get back double in return. What we said is gone is truly never far away. What we lend today we in turn borrow tomorrow's bread.

Though we weep tonight, we do find ourselves awakening to rejoice with the first morning's light. Though we've lost the fight, the battle's already won. Though it seems we're pinned down, we've already overcome. Though it seems that we are forsaken, we are not cast down. Though it seems we are defeated, we are not utterly destroyed. Though it seems we're perplexed, we have peace within the storm. Though the mountain move and the earth be shaken, we are hidden deep within His breast. We have a sure foundation, though our feet stumble beneath us; we are held steadfast within the safety of His arms, secured in the Rock who is the Lord.

So ask yourselves this question: when shall I let go? If we say on Him all our cares we've cast completely, if we say He is our fortress, our buckler, and our shield, if we say in Him, we put our trust, then none other will we yield, if all to Him we've surrendered, then in Christ the Lord we will live. If we say He is a lamp unto our path, then he'll be our guide, a light unto our feet. If we let go of our mind, our strength, our will to Him, then the Lord with His Holy Spirit can truly fill every area of our lives.

> *We are troubled on every side, yet not distressed: we are perplexed, but not in despair; ^Persecuted, but not forsaken; cast down, but not destroyed; 2Cor 4:8. 9 – 5.3

Remember, today is right now, what we see, what we know, and what we hold—the present. Yesterday is that which from us has already slipped away—the past. And tomorrow is that which is yet to come—the future. And it's not promised to us. Know that while in the breaches of loss, there is a hand that comforts—a friend that calms, cares, and cheers, a voice so soothing that it's like music to the ears. This voice reaches out and says, "Let it go and let God!"

Loss can only be driven out when
fueled by tomorrow's dreams
Partake in today's celebration, release
from yesterday's pain.
The past is the past; we must forgive
if we ourselves will live
We see the hope of surrendering our
losses and capturing all our gains
When we ourselves surrender to Jesus Christ, the King.

(Sharon M. Stone)

CHAPTER 8

VICTORY IN JESUS!

Overcoming a Defeat Killer

You've heard or seen Capital One's commercial; their tagline asks, "What's in your wallet?" The thought process here is to help you to overcome high interest rates and little service from the other credit card companies with their comprehensive package that's full of savings, options, and values. Their dramatization using rustic Vikings (barbarians) sends a message that you can conquer those high rates if you carry Capital One. Well, when it comes to overcoming, here's a question for you, "What's in your testimony?" Really, what does your testimony say about you? Is it one of utter failure, disappointment, and defeat? Or one of triumphant victory? You don't have to have a defeatist attitude! Trust in Jesus to bring you through it, to strengthen you because of it, to empower you with it, to edify you by it, and to transform you in the midst of it. Do we whine or complain when we go through or have to deal with the unpleasantries of life? They're called storms (trials, tribulations, or tests), and Jesus said that in this life we would have them.

In the last chapter, we briefly discuss overcoming. Here I will elaborate on it in more depth. There are so many wonderful benefits of being an overcomer. I'd like to address one. Did you realize that your overcoming kills defeat? Even when the enemy thinks he's got you right where he wants you, you can still come out the overcomer and triumphant conqueror. When it seems you're leveled or suppressed (crushed) to the ground, by looking up you change your whole perspective, then you'll be able to see where your hope and help comes from.

As the psalmist wrote, "I WILL lift up mine eyes unto the hills, from whence cometh my help. My help cometh from the Lord, which made heaven and earth" *(Ps. 121:1-2, SPIB)*.

But what does it means when we say we overcame? It is defined by *Webster* like this:

> 1: to get the better of: CONQUER 2: to make helpless or exhausted: beat, defeat, master, prevail over and surmount; subdue.

This is what God told Adam to do in the garden. According to His word, God intended for us to be conquerors from the beginning. God gave us dominion over all that He created upon the earth.

> And God blessed them, and God said unto them, Be fruitful, and multiply, and replenish the earth, and subdue it: and have dominion over the fish of the sea, and over the fowl of the air, and over every living thing that moveth upon the earth. *(Gen. 1:28, KJV)*

God entrusted and endowed us with authority, liberty, creativity, multiplication, and peace. He positioned us above every living thing. He placed us in a rich productive environment with only one adversary, only one to subdue.

> Subdue \ vb sub-dued; subduing 1: to conquer and bring into subjection 2: to bring under control: CURB 3: to reduce the intensity of. Conquer, dominate, overpower, subject, vanquish *(Merriam-Webster's Dictionary)*

In the beginning our flesh was not our problem. Man walked with God at the cool of the day. We did so until sin entered the garden. Adam didn't realize that one act of disobedience would cause his whole world to spiral out of control. Adam didn't foresee that by not conquering his foe, his foe would cause not only his downfall but the downfall of all humanity. Perhaps it was almost impossible to believe there was something that needed to be conquered because God placed man in the most tranquil, calm, and serene dwelling: the Garden of Eden. This omission to heed all of God's word cost us our original purpose, position, provision, and habitat. It removed us from God's original plan for us: living, loving, and walking (communing, fellowshipping) with Him forever without sin. With one act of disobedience, we went from being conquerors to being conquered, from being victorious to being victims, from being masters of all God's goodness to being subservient servants of sin. This happens when our eyes are full of harlotry and are insatiable for sin. That's when we are enslaved by it. This is liberty perverted and defiled. *(See Prov. 26:11.)*

> They promise them liberty, when they themselves are the slaves of depravity and defilement—for by whatever anyone is made inferior or worse or is overcome, to that [person or thing] he is enslaved. For if, after they have escaped the pollutions of the world through [the full, personal] knowledge of our Lord and Savior Jesus Christ, they again become entangled in them and are overcome, their last condition is worse [for them] than the first. There has befallen them the thing spoken of in the true proverb, The dog turns back to his own vomit, and, The sow is washed only to wallow again in the mire. *(2 Pet. 2:19-20, 22, AMP)*

What helps me to overcome? The word of God (Jesus), the living bread. He equips us with His Spirit to overcome. When adversity or the adversary comes, just step over with the word! To overcome means to come over.

> For the Word that God speaks is alive and full of power [making it active, operative, energizing, and effective]; it is sharper than any two-edged sword, penetrating to the dividing line of the breath of life (soul) and [the immortal] spirit, and of joints and marrow [of the deepest parts of our nature], exposing and sifting and analyzing and judging the very thoughts and purposes of the heart. *(Heb. 4:12, AMP)*

Knowing or having a relationship with Jesus and conforming to the image and likeness of God is key, abiding in the Lord and he abiding in us. It is imperative that we have a relationship with God where we attend to His voice and follow the leading of the Holy Spirit if we desire to conquer or subdue our adversary, the devil, along with all his wiles (devices).

> I have written unto you fathers, because ye have known him that is from the beginning. I have written unto you, young men, because ye are strong, and the word of God abideth in you, and ye have overcome the wicked one. *(1 John 2:14, KJV)*

> For the god of this world has blinded the unbelievers' minds [that they should not discern the truth], preventing them from seeing the illuminating light of the Gospel of the glory of Christ (the Messiah), Who is the Image and Likeness of God. *(2 Cor. 4:4, AMP)*

This is not being blinded by the god of this world: We overcome when our mind is focused and centered on Christ. That's why we must subject our minds to Him. We must take on the mind of Christ.

> Let this mind be in you which was also Christ Jesus. *(Phil. 2:5, KJV)*

> [Inasmuch as we] refute arguments and theories and reasonings and every proud and lofty thing that sets itself up against the [true] knowledge of God; and we lead every thought and purpose away captive into the obedience of Christ (the Messiah, the Anointed One). *(2 Cor. 10:5, AMP)*

Thank you Lord for empowering and transforming my mind!

Overcoming through Love

When thinking about overcoming, I'm reminded of this thought: overcame is in the past tense, and overcoming is here and now. It takes the love of Christ to help us come out victorious! Apostle Paul declared that we are more than conquerors through the love of Christ. He reminded us that we as believers have this blessed assurance in Christ Jesus, the Hope of Glory.

> As it is written: "For Your sake we a re killed all day long;
> We are accounted as sheep for the slaughter." Yet in all these
> things we are more than conquerors through Him who loved us.
> *(Rom. 8:36-37, NKJV-SSB)*

It is the same love that the Lord our God and heavenly Father had for us in the garden, that, though we had lost our position and purpose, he would redeem and reconcile us back to Him. He would reposition, reassign, and restore us in right fellowship with Him. It is that same love that caused God to give his Son as the supreme sacrifice for all our sins and purchase us back through the shedding of His blood. Glory to God! It is because of His great love we are now made conquerors!

This is what His love did and does for us:

With God's perfect (complete, full) love, we overcome fear. With His (unspeakable) joy, we overcome sorrow. With His peace (that passes understanding), we overcome disturbances of all kinds, whether of the spirit, soul, body, or mind. With His fruit of the Spirit, we overcome the works of the flesh. We overcome the spirit of heaviness with the garments of praise. With His temperance (self-control) and godly conduct, we overcome uncontrolled behavior (being out of control). With prayer and fasting, we overcome the works of the devil. We overcome sin and its penalty when we receive the finished work of redemption through the Lord and Savior, Jesus Christ. His life, death, burial, and resurrection guarantee us this assured victory. With the blood of the Lamb and our testimony, we overcome the evil one, and it all works through God's agape (unconditional) love working and being active in us. The blood of Jesus causes us to overcome!

Look at John 3:16 NKJV-SSB, which says,

> For God so loved the world that He gave His only begotten
> Son, that whoever believes in Him should not perish but have
> everlasting life.

God's amazing love for us was so great that He gave us life everlasting through His Son. With His atoning sacrifice we were made clean, redeemed by the blood of the Lamb. When we believe in Jesus, we overcome the penalty of sin, which is death. We move from being slaves of sin to being sons of liberty through Christ Jesus, our Lord! We become children of life and not children of death. We are made heirs of salvation instead of heirs of damnation. Hallelujah! Thank you, Lord, for making us overcomers through Your love!

> The Father loves the Son, and has given all things into His hand. He who believes in the Son has everlasting life; and he who does not believe the Son shall not see life, but the wrath of God abides on him. *(John 3: 35-36, NKJV-SSB)*

Victory in Jesus!

What is *victory*? It is defined by *Merriam-Webster* this way:

> 1: the overcoming of an enemy or an antagonist 2: achievement of mastery or success in a struggle or endeavor

We gain the victory when we overcome the world (this age system), and we have overcome because Christ Jesus came to destroy or render null and void the works of the devil. Satan is the god of this world's crooked, evil system. It is influenced by Satan. But Christ Jesus is our champion. He crushed asunder those works (devices, tactics, plots, ploys, and the like), making them powerless before Him.

> He who sins is of the devil, for the devil sinned from the beginning. For this purpose the Son of God was manifested, that He might destroy the works of the devil. *(1 John 3:8, NKJV-SSB)*

See also John 16:33.

> For whatever is born of God overcomes the world. And this is the victory that has overcome the world our faith. *(1 John 5:4, NKJV-SSB)*

I desire to take a little moment to reflect on what victory means to me. As we peer into the pages of the victor's song and grasp the vision of victories past, we will see the future of our greatest victory, which was won so long ago. Through the resurrection power of our Savior, Lord, and King. Through the awesome orchestration of His divine power, he proclaimed our victory sweet as with each word He sealed Satan's defeat.

> "I am the Alpha and Omega, the Beginning and the End," says the Lord, "who is and was and who is to come, the Almighty." *(Rev. 1:8, NKJV-SSB)*

> And when I saw Him, I fell at His feet as dead. But He laid His right hand on me, saying to me, Do not be afraid; I am the First and the Last. I am He who lives, and was dead, and behold I am alive forevermore. Amen. And I have the keys of Hades [hell] and of Death." *(Rev. 1:17-18, KJV-SSB)*

Amen. And I have the keys of Hades [hell] and of Death." *(Rev. 1:17-18, NKJV-SSB)*

Victory means to conquer, to overcome, to overtake, and to subdue one's opponent or foe and one's trials and tribulation too, just like how the violent takes a kingdom by force. As we look through God's word, we see blessed evidence of how we are made more than conquerors through Him that loves us (Rom. 8:28-37). We have the victory of being overcomers! There are three witnesses in heaven, as well as three on the earth, to testify to this.

> For there are three that bear witness in heaven: the Father, the Word, and the Holy Spirit; and these three are one. And there are three that bear witness on earth: the Spirit, the water, and the blood; and these three agree as one. *(1 John 5:7-8, NKJV-SSB)*

We are victorious through the blood of the Lamb and the word of our own testimony, as the scripture says. Oh saints, haven't you read Revelation 12:10-11? We have the victory for we can say that we've been redeemed and we have forgiveness from our Father above.

> He has delivered us from the power of darkness and conveyed us into the kingdom of the Son of His love, in whom we have redemption through His blood, the forgiveness of sins. *(Col 1:13-14, NKJV-SSB)*

I am reminded of the old hymnal song by E. M. Bartlett called "Victory in Jesus." It tells of our lives being made triumphant through Jesus, our Lord, and how He made it possible for us to conquer whatever comes our way that would prevent us from living victoriously. It speaks about the cleansing power of His blood and how it will and can change our lives forever if we trust Him, if we surrender to Him. I truly love that we don't have to live defeated or overpowered or enslaved by anything or anyone, that we can be free in Jesus! Absorb to these words. Let them take root in your heart today:

> I heard an old story, how a Savior came from glory, How He gave his life on Calvary to save a wretch like me; I heard about His groaning, of His precious blood's atoning; Then I repented of my sins and won the victory.

> I heard about His healing, of His cleansing power revealing, How He made the lame to walk again and caused the blind to

see; And then I cried "Dear Jesus, come and heal my broken spirit," And somehow Jesus came and bro't to me the victory.

I heard about a mansion he has built for me in glory, And I heard about the streets of gold beyond the crystal sea; About the angels singing, and the old redemption story, And some sweet day I'll sing up there the song of victory.

Chorus: O victory in Jesus, my Savior forever, He sought me and bro't me with His redeeming blood; He loved me ere I knew Him, and all my love is due Him, He plunged me to victory, beneath the cleansing flood.

There's no mistake. Come and partake, then you too will have victory through the blood of Jesus. We are victorious because He has made provisions for us in this manner, even as it were foretold by the prophet Isaiah that no weapon formed, created, or developed against us would prosper (Isa. 54:17). We are victorious because through Christ we are made free by his truth.

Now the Lord is that Spirit; and where the Spirit of the Lord is, there is liberty. But we are all, with unveiled face, beholding as in a mirror the glory of the Lord, are being transformed into the same image from glory to glory, just as by the Spirit of the Lord. *(2 Cor. 3:17-18, NKJV-SSB)*

Therefore, if anyone is in Christ, he is a new creation; old things have passed away; behold, all things have become new. *(2 Cor. 5:17, NKJV)*

And you shall know the truth, and the truth shall make you free...Therefore if the Son makes you free, you shall be free indeed. *(John 8:32, 36, NKJV)*

STAND fast therefore in the liberty by which Christ has made us free, and do not be entangled again with the yoke of bondage. *(Gal. 5:1, SPLB)*

We are victorious because we're empowered by His Holy Spirit to do all things, even to be witnesses. We are victorious by living our lives through Him. Though we were dead in sins, by the washing of Jesus's blood, we are made alive, redeemed, reborn, and revived as lively stones. Therefore we can live life victoriously!

I can do all things through Christ who strengthens me. *(Phil. 4:13, NKJV)*

But you shall receive power when the Holy Spirit has come upon you; and you shall be witnesses to Me in Jerusalem, and in all Judea and Samaria, and to the end of the earth. *(Acts 1:8, NKJV)*

I have been crucified with Christ; it is no longer I who live, but Christ lives in me; and the life which I now live in the flesh I live by faith in the Son of God, who loved me and gave Himself for me. *(Gal. 2:20, NKJV-SSB)*

It is from the beginning that our God blessed us when he made us subdue the whole earth for we were and are the express image of His presence. Genesis 1:28 instills this, that God planned for us to be fully equipped with His power and to live victoriously through Him.

There Is Victory in Jesus!

But thanks be to God, which giveth us the victory through our Lord Jesus Christ. *(1 Cor. 15:57, KJV)*

To close out this chapter, I would like to share with you the wonderful benefits of being an overcomer or overcoming (he that overcometh). Jesus promised to reward us for overcoming as He has overcome:

1. We'll eat from the tree of life.

   He who has an ear, let him hear what the Spirit says to the churches. To him who overcomes I will give to eat from the tree of life, which is in the midst of the Paradise of God. *(Rev. 2:7, NKJV-SSB)*

2. We'll escape the second death.

   He who has an ear, let him hear what the Spirit says to the churches. He who overcomes shall not be hurt by the second death. *(Rev. 2:11, NKJV-SSB)*

3. We'll receive a new name.

   He who has an ear, let him hear what the Spirit says to the churches. To him who overcomes I will give some of the hidden manna to eat. And I will give him a white stone, and on the stone a new name written which no one knows except him who receives it. *(Rev. 2:17, NKJV-SSB)*

4. We'll receive power over the nations.

   And he who overcomes, and keeps My works until the end, to him I will give power over the nations—...as I received from My Father; and I will give him the morning star. He who has an ear, let him hear what the Spirit says to the churches." *(Rev. 2:26-29, NKJV)*

5. We'll be clothed in white.

   He who overcomes shall be clothed in white garments, and I will not blot his name from the Book of Life; but I will confess his name before My Father and before his angels. He who has an ear, let him hear what the Spirit says to the churches. *(Rev. 3:5-6, NKJV)*

6. We'll be a pillar in God's temple.

   He who overcomes, I will make him a pillar in the temple of My God, and he shall go out no more. I will write on him the name of MY God, the New Jerusalem, which comes down out of heaven from My God. And I will write on him My new name. He who has an ear, let him hear what the Spirit says to the churches. *(Rev. 3:12-13, NKJV)*

7. We'll sit with Jesus on his throne.

   To him who overcomes I will grant to sit with Me on My throne, as I also overcame and sat down with My Father on His throne. He who has an ear, let him hear what the Spirit says to the churches." *(Rev. 3:21-22, NKJV)*

8. We shall be God's sons.

   He who overcomes shall inherit all things, and I will be his God and he shall be My son. *(Rev. 21:7, NKJV)*

Therefore, whatever it is that has held you bound and captive and every time you turned the corner, you are constantly reminded of the scene of your hurt or pain, I like to encourage you today to give it up! Turn it over to the Lord. You can't handle it alone. Don't succumb to your fears. Have faith in God! Give it to the One who sits upon the throne forever, the King of Glory. Let Him into your life. Cast all your burdens, cares, woes, or griefs upon Jesus for he cares for you. There is victory in Jesus! Let Him wash you, wipe away your tears, bind up every wound for the Lord gives beauty for ashes, the oil of joy for sorrows, and the garments of praise for the spirit of heaviness. Trust in the Lord, and he will bring it to pass. And when you do this, you'll know for yourself that He heals the hurt!

My Prayer for You

Father God, I beseech you by your loving-kindness and tender mercies. Lord, I pray for each individual who has read or will read the pages of this book, that as they take this journey from hurt to healing, they will be released forever from the anguish of the hurt that has gripped their lives. I pray that through Your word, love, and Spirit, they'll know that You can and will erase their pain and make them fully whole.

Father, I praise you for deliverance and setting us free through your holy child, Jesus Christ, who, through the finished work of redemption, brought to us restoration and reconciliation, making us a new creation in You.

Now, Lord God of Israel, verify the word in each individual's life that You by your Holy Spirit have given me to pen upon these pages. Lord, let every word of healing be lively stones, transforming, renewing, and saturating the hearts and minds of the people. To the Only wise God be glory, honor, and praise both now and forevermore in the precious atoning name of Jesus. Amen!

INVITATION TO LIFE EVERLASTING

Let me offer you the opportunity to begin your transformation today by offering the best invitation you will ever receive that will impact your life forever. If you haven't received Jesus as your personal Lord and Savior, I'd like to invite you do so now! Romans 6:23 (KJV) says, "For the wages of sin is death; but the gift of God is eternal life." Ask Jesus to come into your life today and heal the hurt. Ask Him to fill your heart, every void and empty place with His love, peace, joy, and His Holy Spirit. The Bible says in Romans 10:9-10, 13 (AMP),

> Because if you acknowledge and confess with your lips that Jesus is Lord and, in your heart, believe (adheres to, trust in, and rely on the truth) that God has raised Him from the dead, you will be saved. For with the heart a person believes (adheres to, trusts in, and relies on Christ) and so is justified (declared righteous, acceptable to God), and with the mouth he confesses (declares openly and speaks out freely his faith) and confirms [his] salvation...For everyone who calls upon the name of the Lord [invoking Him as Lord] shall be saved.

Declare it now. I acknowledge and confess now that Jesus is Lord and believe in my heart that you, Lord God have raised him from the dead; therefore, I am saved! Do you believe this? If so, let me be the first to welcome you now into the family of God!

Are you out of fellowship with the Lord and missing the closeness you've once shared? You can be restored this very moment. All you have to do is come!

In 1 John 1:7, 9 (AMP), it says,

> And the blood of Jesus Christ his Son cleanses (removes) us from all sin and guilt [keeps us cleansed from sin in all its forms and manifestations]. If we [freely] admit that we have sinned and confess our sins, He is faithful and just (true to His own nature and promises) and will forgive our sins [dismiss our lawlessness] and [continuously] cleanse us from all unrighteousness [everything not in conformity to His will in purpose, thought, and action].

Believe this as you surrender it all to Him today and walk in the light as He is the Light!

ABOUT THE AUTHOR

Sharon M. Stone
Daughter of the King
Child of the true and living God
Chosen for His purpose

Apostle Sharon (Lady Beckford) Stone was born March 6, 1961, in the township of Waterworks, Frankfield, thirteen miles outside of Ocho Rios, Jamaica, West Indies, down in the Caribbean. She was brought here through the ministry of her father (Bishop Vincent S. Beckford Sr., senior pastor of Georgian Hills Church of God), and here is where it all began for her. She received Jesus as Lord and Savior at the age of eight. When she was nine, she truly had a Pentecostal experience when she received the baptism of the Holy Ghost. (Back then they'd fasted, prayed, and waited on the Lord until they received).

It is her deepest and most heartfelt desire to give God the glory in all she does and say, with all her being, whether it be in words, song, action, or deeds, to become that which she now does behold (His glory), to be made the vessel of the Master's divine choosing for his use, to use those gifts that He has given her to reach a lost and dying world whenever, wherever, and however the Lord her God shall desire to use them. She declares, "Forsaking all, I take Him!"

She is saved by the blood of the Lamb, sanctified by the precious Word of God, filled with his precious Holy Ghost, and drenched with His fire. She is rooted and grounded in Jesus Christ, who is her solid foundation whereupon she does stand. She has received her adoption into God's holy family, being made an heir of the Father and a joint heir with the Son, taking unto her His divine nature whereby she can cry "Abba, Father" and remain in His love. She has received the distinct pleasure of being directed, taught, breathed on, and guided by the Holy Spirit, who has led her into the deep mysteries of God. She has been chosen, brought with a price, loved because He first loved her, justified because of the cross, esteemed (promoted, uplifted, raised up) because He exalts the man of low estate.

He calls her an author. Since September 24, 1984, He, the Rock that's higher than us, gave her a golden inkhorn. He turned her ability to write into a gift with one word the Holy Spirit spoke to her that blessed morning—write! It was like a ton of bricks and a sledgehammer coming down on her all at the same time, and she's been writing every since.

Apostle Sharon Stone is an illustrious, prolific poet with International Poet Society and Noble House of London, 2008-2009, and an honored member of Biltmore Who's Who as well. She currently works in the church as teacher of the Word, a worship leader singing and giving God the praise, a preacher of the Word in the media ministry, and a bearer of the cross. As a minister of God, she meets the needs of the people through intercessory prayer, pulling down strongholds of the devil, praying without ceasing.

She's a wonderful mother and nurturing NaNa (grandmother). She is anointed for service, drenched in God's love to preach his love and grace, covered by His blood, steeped in prayer, empowered by His Holy Spirit, called, chosen, and appointed for a time such as this!

The mission is clear, and the pathway is free of obstruction. The Lord himself has spoken, decreed, and called this thing to be. The mandate of the Lord for this mighty outpouring of his resurrection power is assured because it is He that ordained it, he that sustains it, he that makes it manifests!

REFERENCES

Merriam-Webster's Dictionary and Thesaurus, Copyright © 2006 by Merriam-Webster Inc.

Strong's Exhaustive Concordance of the Bible with Greek and Hebrew Dictionary theInterviewwithgod.com

MemphisFacts.com

Familysafemedia.com

Rainn.org

Handguns and Children: A Lethal Combination

StoptheViolence-EngridMalone Jun 10,2009BVITALENT.com/index.php?stop-the-violence...poems

Dictionary.com, theFreedictionary.com